THE BIG GAME

ALSO BY TIM GREEN

FOOTBALL GENIUS NOVELS

Football Genius
Football Hero
Football Champ
The Big Time
Deep Zone
Perfect Season
Left Out

BASEBALL GREAT NOVELS

Baseball Great
Rivals
Best of the Best
Home Run

AND DON'T MISS

Pinch Hit
Force Out
Unstoppable
New Kid
First Team
Kid Owner
Touchdown Kid

THE BIG GAME

TIM GREEN

HARPER

An Imprint of HarperCollinsPublishers

Library of Congress Cataloging-in-Publication Data

Names: Green, Tim, author.
Title: The big game / Tim Green.
Description: First edition. | New York, NY : Harper, an imprint of
HarperCollinsPublishers, [2018] | Summary: Danny Owens is dedicating his
seventh-grade football season to his recently deceased father, an NFL
legend, but the pressure to succeed is magnified by his inability to read.
Identifiers: LCCN 2018013363 | ISBN 9780062485045 (hardback)
Subjects: | CYAC: Football—Fiction. | Junior high schools—Fiction. |
Schools—Fiction. | Literacy—Fiction. | Counseling—Fiction. | Fathers
and sons—Fiction. | Family life—Texas—Fiction. | Texas—Fiction. |
BISAC: JUVENILE FICTION / Sports & Recreation / Football. | JUVENILE
FICTION / Social Issues / Special Needs. | JUVENILE FICTION / Action &
Adventure / General.
Classification: LCC PZ7.G826357 Bid 2018 | DDC [Fic]—dc23 LC record available
at https://lccn.loc.gov/2018013363

Typography by Kate Engbring
18 19 20 21 22   CG/LSCH   10 9 8 7 6 5 4 3 2 1
❖
First Edition

For my Six Angels . . . I'm right here with you. Always.

THE BIG GAME

The three friends lay side by side with Danny in the middle. The floor of their tree house was triangular. It worked out okay because Janey fit near the wall, under the window. Danny was a big kid for twelve, but he went in the middle because Cupcake took up the most space. Cupcake was enormous and his legs extended through the open trapdoor. He was built like a small refrigerator, with square shoulders and jaw, a flattop haircut, meaty hands, and ears flatter to his head than a coonhound. He looked like he'd been assembled from a giant Lego set. The only thing small about Cupcake were his teeth, which spilled around the inside of his mouth like corn off the cob.

"After your first four years in the NFL, you become a free agent," Danny explained. "So even if we don't get drafted by the same team, we can go wherever we want after four years."

"Pittsburgh?" Cupcake suggested, brushing light brown

hair out of his pale blue eyes.

Danny frowned. "I'm not my dad, Cupcake. When will you get that through your head?"

"Who wouldn't want to be your dad?" Cupcake grumbled. "Only you."

Danny wanted to change the subject. "I think we'll let Janey decide where we go."

Janey smiled.

"Janey?" Cupcake sat up and looked down at Danny with a frown.

"Yeah," Danny said. "By then she'll be a doctor and she'll have to pick where she wants to do her residency. Wherever that is, we can go play for that team."

Cupcake's face still hovered above them. "What if the team stinks? Like, Cleveland or something?"

"Janey wouldn't want to go anyplace with a lousy team," Danny said.

"For sure." Janey spoke in a dreamy voice, almost like she'd been dozing off.

"Oh." Cupcake lay back down. "I wish it would cool off. I swear, four o'clock is the hottest part of the day."

Danny bolted up. "Wait, it's not four yet."

"It's three minutes after four." Cupcake held up his phone.

"No. I set an alarm." Danny fumbled with his own phone and saw he'd set it for 3:30 *a.m.* "Oh, shiitake mushrooms!"

Danny scrambled up, pushed Cupcake's legs aside, and scrambled down the ladder.

Janey's face appeared in the window above. "Where you going?"

Danny turned and ran, shouting over his shoulder. "My dad's work! He's taking me for football cleats!"

He flew through the woods, down a long winding path that came out by the guardrail on Route 222. He scooped his bike out of the tall grass and rocketed into Crooked Creek.

Shops in town had already changed their Fourth of July red-white-and-blue banners and flags for football banners and bunting—purple and white for the Crooked Creek Junior High Raiders, gold and black for the Jericho High Cowboys. The clock over the old brick corner store showed how late he was. He turned left at the store and pedaled like a madman to the edge of town, where the enormous showroom of Zurich Farm Implements dominated the street. In the front of the three-story glass showroom window was a bright red combine the size of a dinosaur.

Danny ditched his bike near the service entrance and entered the showroom from the back. The first floor was lined with offices of the salesmen who worked under his dad. There were seven other stores across the state with their own stables of salesmen who also worked for Danny's dad. Danny waved at Mr. Humphrys through his office window and took the stairs two at a time up to his father's large glass office overlooking the showroom. He rounded the corner and froze.

Sitting across from his father's desk was the hulking figure of a farmer wearing a plaid shirt and suspenders. Danny's dad saw him, and instead of giving Danny the scowl he expected for being late, he grinned and waved his son in. Danny obeyed.

"Mr. Lindsey, this is my son, Danny."

"Sorry I'm late, Dad."

"Mr. Lindsey, are kids ever on time?"

"Not like you and me ever were." The farmer stood up and extended a leathery hand to Danny. "I heard you're a chip off the block. Gonna lead Crooked Creek to the county championship this season, people are sayin'."

"I hope so, sir."

"Even looks like you, Daniel." The farmer squinted at Danny's dad. "We'll see if he gets that ring you got, though. If he's like my kids, he won't. My kids want to play in a rock band. A *rock band*. I'm ashamed to say it, and me with thirty thousand acres."

"That's why you've got me, Dave." Danny's dad thumped his chest before rounding his desk and putting an arm around the man. "These new combines practically run themselves."

"That'll be a comfort when I'm in my grave."

Danny's dad gave a hearty laugh. "Well, this is some deal for us both, Dave, and I appreciate your business. I've seen a man or two go over to the Kubota dealer in Dustville."

"Pshaw! Dustville? That ain't even in Jericho County! You won't see me in Dustville. You think the Kubota sales manager won them a state title? You think he's got one o' them rings?" The farmer pointed to Danny's father's right hand, where a giant, bejeweled Super Bowl ring glinted in the light.

"Well, thank you, Dave. Thank you very much." Danny's father dipped his head as if embarrassed.

"You see that, son?" The farmer scowled at Danny like he'd done much more wrong than being late. "That's why this town—heck, this whole part of the state—loves your daddy. He coulda stayed in Pittsburgh. A Super Bowl winner? He coulda done whatever he wanted, but he's a good ole Texas boy, and humble too. Not like those ninny-hammered showboats you see on TV today. You'd be best served to follow this man's footprints, son, step for step, an' that's comin' from a man with thirty thousand acres."

The farmer was quite worked up, and Danny hung his head as if to apologize for all wrongdoers, but he didn't mean it. He was tired of this game.

"Okeydokey, Dave. Now I gotta get the boy to the shoe store for some cleats, then back home for his momma's supper on time, so we'll be seein' you."

They saw Dave to the stairs before Danny's dad wheeled him past the owner's office. Mr. Zurich sat at a big desk wearing a bow tie with his sleeves rolled up, amid a pile of paper.

Danny's dad ducked his head inside. "I'm gone, boss. Gotta get Danny's football cleats."

The owner whipped off his glasses. "Danny? You take those Raiders to the championship, boy. People sayin' good things about you maybe bein' as good as your dad. That I'll have to see, no offense, son."

Danny shook his head as if none were taken.

"Looks like you, don't he, Daniel?" Mr. Zurich smiled, showing a line of perfect white teeth that didn't match the deep lines in his craggy face.

"More an' more, boss, more an' more."

Danny waved like his dad and off they went.

In the car, the radio played a country song about a boy and his dad, and Danny felt like pulling his hair out. He loved his dad, it wasn't that. And he was proud of the way everyone waved at his truck as they drove through town or stopped him on the street to look at the ring, or how his dad got to be on the sideline with a select few Jericho alumni for the varsity games.

It was that Danny wanted to be *himself*.

And in this town, he just didn't know if that was possible.

The box of new white cleats rested in their bag at Danny's feet.

"Thank you," Danny said. "For the cleats."

"You said thanks already—twice."

"I know. Just wanted to make sure you knew."

His dad pulled onto State Route 414 before he gripped Danny's knee. The ring's many diamonds sparkled in a beam of late-day sun. "You're a good kid, Danny. I'm not just saying that because of the way you play football. You got good manners and you're smart."

"Tell my teachers that," Danny scoffed. His grades were up and down, mostly down recently.

"Don't worry about teachers and all that school stuff. Look at me. You play in the league, you'll be all set. You don't got to be book smart, just *playbook* smart. And you're people smart, like me. You know how much equipment I sold Dave Lindsey today?"

"No, sir."

"Seven million dollars' worth." His dad gave Danny a glance and Danny's mouth dropped open. "Yeah, commission on that'll buy a new roof and pay for a huge vacation. But I had to work my way up to that spot. I started down on the ground floor like everyone else. What I'm saying is that me being gone all summer is for a reason."

"Yes, sir."

"But I'm fixin' to spend some more time home now the season's comin'. I got to be there for you. I been through all this."

"Yes, sir."

His dad messed his hair and turned up the radio. Lee Brice was singing "I Drive Your Truck." His dad's voice boomed as they both sang along. When it was over, Danny's dad had tears in his eyes, something that never happened. His dad got a sour look on his face and scowled at the road so long that Danny wondered if his eyes had been playing tricks on him.

The radio's harsh beeping—an emergency warning—distracted them both. A tornado was coming. They looked up at the sky.

"Nothin' so far," his dad said.

When they got home, the sun in the west dipped quickly behind a dark bank of clouds on the horizon.

"Maybe that's it." His dad pointed. "We'll see. It'll be what it'll be, right?"

"Yes, sir."

"Let's throw the ball around, break in those new cleats

while your mom makes us dinner."

"I'll be right out!" Danny ran in past his mom and changed into the new cleats, and then he hightailed it back outside. He and his dad threw and caught and threw some more until the sky was dark.

"Time to wash up and eat," his dad said.

They headed in against wind kicking grit from the driveway into their faces.

Outside the kitchen window, the black sky twisted and moaned. Rain spattered the glass and lightning flashed like a loose bulb on a bad wire. Amid the crash of thunder and the bickering his parents had gotten into ten minutes earlier, Danny drank his milk and listened for the sound of a train. That was the sound he worried about. That's when you really needed to hide in the basement under a thick beam. When the sky made that train sound, a tornado was coming.

"Son!" Danny's father scowled at him from across the table. "Did you not hear me?"

Danny shook his head. "No, sir. I was thinkin'."

"I said you need to get your butt running. Practice is just two weeks out and you've done nothin' except play video games and fool with Janey all summer. This is a big year for you, son. This is *the* year."

"*The* year." Smiling now, Danny's mother shook her head. "Every year's *the* year to you, Daniel. Ever since we were just kids. But if you ask me, there was only one year I'd call *the* year."

Danny's mom aimed her fork out into the living room, where the framed photo of her husband, sweat-drenched and holding the Lombardi Trophy, rested atop the pinewood mantel. "That year in Pittsburgh . . ."

Danny's father growled. "You gotta get there, Sharon. He needs to be the one who jumps out at Coach Oglethorpe come the big game."

Danny's father finished off his can of beer and slapped it down beside his place at the round table before locking eyes with Danny. His father's eyes swirled like the storm outside and Danny knew he was about to hear a story he'd heard many times before. Yet he knew to pay attention. He'd seen his dad charm folks time after time with the story. And he knew how to be polite and act like this was the first time he'd heard it.

"That's when it happened for me." His father stuck a thumb in his own chest before cracking open a fresh can of beer. "Seventh grade. We played Burnside in the county championship game. Coach Sutton—it was Coach Sutton back then—he saw me run for two hundred eighteen yards and punch it into the end zone five times. *Five.* We won that thing, and who do you think got the invite to play on the Jericho High varsity team as an eighth grader?"

"You?" Danny said, knowing his part in the story.

"Yeah, me. All-county freshman year. Second team all-state as a sophomore. First team junior year. All-American as a senior and a five-star recruit. Five stars, that's when everyone and their brother wants you."

Danny's father looked at his mother and his face softened. "Your mom was the prettiest gal in Texas and she wanted me, too."

She was happy to take up the memory. "We were in Pittsburgh with the Steelers for six years, including his world championship season." Danny hoped she wouldn't start on how much she still wanted to be there instead of back here in this country town.

Danny's father looked successful. He was proud of his height and his looks, and of his strength. Still, if you just saw him without knowing, it would be hard to imagine he'd run for 103 yards and punched in two touchdowns in the Super Bowl. His job for Zurich Farm Implements called for lots of travel and entertaining, and at just over six feet tall, he'd taken on weight, most of it in his belly.

"So tomorrow morning it's you and me," Danny's father said to him, getting back to business. "Road work. First light."

Danny's mother made a noise that was halfway between a laugh and a snort. "Since when have you gotten up at dawn to *run*?"

"You got no idea, Sharon. You were painting your toenails by your daddy's pool, getting a suntan, when I was making my way."

Danny felt a knot in his stomach. He hated this bickering. He stabbed the last piece of chicken fried steak on his plate and stuck it into his mouth, chewing fast, all the while thinking he might get an opening where he could ask to be excused.

"That's a pretty high horse you're sittin' on, Sharon, for a wife that never had to work a day in her life. Just shops and buys clothes so she can flirt with every man on Main Street." His father took a big swig of beer and sat back.

His mom smiled with her answer. "I don't flirt with them. They flirt with me."

Then she got serious. "You don't call keeping your clothes nice and putting up with your schedule and taking care of him"—she pointed her fork at Danny—"work?" She stood to begin clearing the table.

"He'd be a darned sight better off carrying a football under his arm than that cell phone you gave him."

"Kids have them, Daniel. How would you like it if we sent him to school with no shoes?"

His father sat still, drumming his thick fingers against the beer can. The wedding band on his father's ring finger made little clicking sounds as Danny got up and began to silently help get the dishes into the kitchen. When a lightning bolt exploded right next to the house, Danny's mom screamed and dropped a plate. It shattered against the kitchen floor as the house plunged into total darkness.

"Now you broke a plate!" yelled his father.

Danny heard his mom digging in the cupboard before the scratch of a match produced a small flame that became a glow as she held it to a candle on the countertop. From the candle, she lit one of her long, thin cigarettes and surrounded herself in a halo of smoke. Tears glistened down her cheeks in the

13

wavering light and she sniffed softly.

"See?" Danny's dad said to him. "What do I always tell you about girls? Waterworks."

With that his mom let out a desperate-sounding sob.

"Oh, now . . ." Danny's father scraped his chair back and engulfed his mother's narrow frame in a bear hug.

Danny retreated down the back hallway to his room, knowing that they would both be fine. They always were. He was grateful for the loss of power, though, because the way they had been going he felt certain more than just a plate was going to be broken. It had happened before.

He checked his phone. The battery was low, so he plugged it in for when the electricity came on and then made a quick call to Janey. She knew everything that happened in their small Texas town. She said that everyone in Crooked Creek had lost power.

He found the flashlight next to his bed without too much trouble because the orange lightning flashes outside his window lit up things pretty good. He looked sadly at his Xbox and then propped the flashlight up on a stack of underwear atop his dresser so that its beam shone down on the desk beside his bed. From the drawer he removed a World War II bomber plane model and started working on it. He could figure out how to put models together without reading the plans. Other military aircraft hung from the ceiling by fishing line, which—especially in the flickering light—gave the impression that a flying armada was circling his bedroom.

Danny hadn't added to his flying collection since his mom had given him the Xbox for his birthday at the beginning of summer along with a twenty-inch flat-screen TV. His dad had been away at a convention looking at new farm equipment. He sure wasn't thrilled when he got home and found out about it, but he had to leave again almost immediately on a sales trip, so he didn't have much time to fuss. Now, if Danny wasn't watching something with his parents, he was playing *Rainbow Six Siege* with Cupcake.

Occasionally, Janey would get on to play *Left 4 Dead 2*. Janey loved the zombies.

The power hadn't returned by the time he grew tired of his bomber. He wandered into the living room, where his parents sat arguing about where to vacation by the light of a battery-powered camping lantern. He said good night and used the flashlight to navigate the bathroom, brush his teeth, and get into bed. He lay for a long while listening for the sound of a train to rise up from the thrum of rain against the roof.

He didn't remember falling asleep, so he had no idea what time of night it was when his father woke him with an edge in his voice.

"Danny! Danny!" His father shook him awake, whispering desperately. "Danny! Now! We've got to go!"

Danny could only think something terrible had happened in the storm. He gulped back the panic bubbling up in the back of his throat.

"Dad? What? What's wrong? Where's Mom?"

"Danny, your mom doesn't need to run three miles. She's still a looker and she knows it. I could lose a few, though. Come on—get up and get dressed. I know I haven't been around much this summer, and I've been letting you down. But your training starts now. Three miles. Let's go."

"Three miles?" Danny sat up and turned his phone on. "Dad, it's five in the morning."

"I know that. Road work. You and me. I told your mom we were starting early, and I meant it. She'll see."

The power must have come back on recently because there was light seeping in from the hallway, and Danny now saw that his father had a new Steelers sweat suit on. Even though it was predawn, his hair was carefully styled and he'd shaved in case folks saw him running.

"Let's go! Let's go!" Danny's father clapped his hands, ready for action.

Danny left his phone plugged in so it could finish charging, then dressed and tied his sneakers. They stepped out onto the front porch, his father quietly pulling the door shut behind them before standing tall and breathing deep.

"How about this air? How fresh is this?"

Everything was wet, but a crisp breeze had cleared away the clouds. The stars winked down at them from a sky that was deep dark blue but no longer black. In the east Danny saw a glow that promised morning.

"Let's walk a bit to loosen things up." Danny's father swung his arms back and forth and then in small circles as they made their way down the long, straight driveway to County Route 222. His father turned right, heading up the hill and away from town.

"See, your mom doesn't understand." His father angled his head back toward the house. "We met in high school, and she doesn't know about this part of it. This part came before her. She doesn't understand that, until now, I've let you just be a kid. You were great on the Pop Warner teams, no doubt about it. A star. But you're twelve years old and going into seventh grade, and this is when things start to get serious. Now, I'm going to ask you a question. What do people say about you in football?"

Danny thought for a moment. "They say . . . I'm tough and I'm fast."

"Yeah, but what else?"

A light went off in Danny's head. "Oh, they say I'm just like you. Another Daniel Owens."

Even in the faint dawn Danny could see his father's smile as he nodded his head. "That's right, another Daniel Owens. You're a chip off the block. You've got everything I have and you can do everything I've done, only you get to do it better."

"Better than you? I don't know about that, Dad."

His father stopped and put a powerful hand on Danny's arm to give him a little shake. "Never doubt yourself. Like I say, you can be better, because you're my son and you've got all my experience to back you up. You never have to doubt yourself, because I'm telling you that you can do this."

Danny nodded, his stomach tightening with the pressure. All his life he'd be Daniel Owens's son.

"And you could be," his father continued, "you *could* be a first-round pick—not third like me. That's why I'm going to train you myself. I'm going to give it everything I've got."

His father gave the big bulge of his stomach a pat. "Not that I couldn't stand to lose a few pounds in the bargain. I know that. You're helping me, I'm helping you. That's why you are going to have a monster season and tear up that championship game, so that Coach Oglethorpe can't *wait* to get you on that varsity team. That's the key. You've got to get up there early, so you get some experience. Then, by the time you're a sophomore in high school, you'll dominate. That's when the colleges will start to drool."

His father extended his hand and Danny grasped it and shook it hard. "Are you with me?"

"Yes," Danny said, and took off after him.

At the top of the hill, his father stopped and pulled him into a rare hug. Danny looked over his dad's shoulder at the lights and the water tower in the little four-corner town of Crooked Creek. He could see Janey's house down the road about a quarter mile from theirs. The front porch light was on, but he imagined Janey and her parents were still asleep like most people in the town. He drew in a breath, feeling special, up here on top of the world in the fresh breeze with his dad, the man he was named after, an NFL player, a world champion.

"That's my boy," his father said, clapping Danny's back before turning him loose.

When his father took off down the other side of the hill on a fast jog, Danny took off too. It felt like flying until the road leveled off on a winding way that more or less followed the creek. They slogged along, heading gradually up again toward the wooded hills in the distance. As the light grew the birds began to wake and sing. It felt so good to be there, just him and his dad and the brand-new day.

Danny didn't know how far they'd gone, but his lungs began to burn and his legs felt like lead. Danny glanced at his father. It looked like he'd been under the garden hose. He was drenched in sweat.

When he began to make sharp wheezing noises, Danny slowed his pace.

"Dad?" Danny huffed and puffed. "Maybe we should turn back?"

His father hung his head like a sleepy bear, but shook it to

19

say no, even though he was struggling to breathe. "Top of . . .
this . . . next hill . . . You always . . . end . . . on top . . . You . . .
gotta . . . push . . ."

His father suddenly gasped and straightened. He clutched
his chest and staggered sideways just off the road.

"Danny?" His father winced like he'd hammered his thumb,
and then he pitched forward and collapsed in the dust.

"Dad!" Danny cried out as he lifted his father's head off the ground.

Reality hit him, and he jumped up and ran home for help.

Somehow, between ragged breaths, he told his mother what had happened. They got back to his dad before the ambulance, and Danny stood, useless, while his mom sat on the roadside with his father's head in her lap. The paramedics arrived and tried to revive him.

Everything else was a blur in Danny's mind. He remembered the sad look on the doctor's face when he told his mom that her husband was gone, and the ghostly sound of her wailing as the doctor assured Danny there was nothing he could have done.

* * *

Everyone in Crooked Creek came to the funeral, and it seemed like half of Jericho County as well. Danny stood there next to his mother, dry eyed. Always lively in a crowd, today she stood stiff, her eyes brimming with tears. The dark suit he wore made him sweat, and the tie made him itch.

The coffin loomed to the side of them, but Danny couldn't bear to look at the big waxy figure that had been his dad.

The endless line of people all seemed to say the same things.

"He was just such a great man."

"Just too young for a heart attack."

"I know you made him so proud, Danny."

"He always told everyone you'd be even better than he was."

"Sorry for your loss, son."

"You look just like him."

"He's gonna live on through you, son."

And Danny replied just the same, no matter what they said. "Yes, sir." "Thank you, ma'am."

Some of the men wore football jerseys—Crooked Creek purple or Jericho gold—beneath their black coats and told brief stories about how his dad had bested them or others on the gridiron. Their memories were just words to Danny, like pebbles rattling in an empty can.

Janey and Cupcake stayed through to the bitter end, until those who had been invited to the house after the burial left.

"Man," Cupcake said, "everyone sure loved your dad. There must have been three thousand people."

"Too bad two thousand nine hundred fifty of them were morons." Danny stretched out his feet and loosened his tie.

"Why?" Cupcake wrinkled his brow.

Danny clenched his sweaty hands. "Football this and football that and 'Oh, you're just like your dad. No, you *are* your dad.' What the heck is that? Why would anyone *say* that? I mean, he's gone. *I'm here.*"

"I'm sure they were only trying to be nice," Janey said quietly.

Danny blinked. "Do you think that's *nice?*"

She put a hand on his shoulder. "I know you, but these people knew your dad. They admired him. I think a lot of them wanted to be him."

Danny felt like someone had him in a bear hug. It was hard to breathe. "But I'm *me*, right?"

Janey grabbed his arm with both hands. "Of course you are, Danny. And you're our best friend in the world."

After they buried his father, after all the people left and a new day was dawning, Danny didn't talk about what had happened. Janey and Cupcake knew him well and never said another word, but they stayed close for the rest of the summer. When he wasn't alone aimlessly riding the mower, he spent his time hanging out with Janey at the creek or playing Xbox with Cupcake. None of it required him to talk.

His mom didn't talk either. She sighed a lot and smoked her thin cigarettes and made dinner for the two of them, which they ate with the TV on. Sometimes she started to cry, but whenever that happened she'd hurry off to her room like she was ashamed.

Danny didn't cry because he didn't let himself think about

what happened. He was just numb. He must have lost track of the days and weeks, too, because he was surprised when, after he and Cupcake defeated a drug lord in the *Ghost Recon* video game, his friend asked, "You ready for tomorrow?"

"What do you mean?" Danny said.

"Football."

"Football?"

"Stop messing with me, Danny. Practice starts tomorrow. You know that." Cupcake huffed.

Danny said, "No. I wasn't thinking."

Their headsets remained quiet for some time before Danny said, "Okay, I gotta go."

He disconnected his headset before Cupcake could reply and got ready for bed.

In the morning, he made himself cinnamon toast before climbing aboard the old John Deere rider mower. They had five acres of lawn. It took him all morning to cut it, because when he got far from the house, he switched off the engine and just sat there with the sun beating down. His dad used to call it the "devil's glare" when it got this hot, the kind of heat that reached your bones.

When he headed back for lunch, he spotted a silver Ford F-150 in the driveway. It was a big truck with giant tires and a chrome grille, and his heart skipped a beat at the thought of another man calling on his mom so soon after his dad had died.

But he could think of no other explanation for the big truck, and a roaring wind started up in his head. Pulling into the garage, he hopped off the mower and wiped the sweat from his forehead. Blind to thought, he grabbed a large wrench from the tool chest and charged into the house through the kitchen door.

When Danny saw the back of a man sitting at the kitchen table cradling a cup of coffee, he raised the wrench.

Coach Kinen spun around in the kitchen chair and spilled his coffee when he saw Danny advancing toward him. He was up on his feet and his voice was low. "Danny, what are you doing?"

Danny stopped short, breathing heavy. The wrench suddenly felt like a fifty-pound weight in his hand and he lowered it to his leg. "I was, uh . . . fixing the mower."

"We missed you at practice this morning." The coach removed his cap and scratched at the balding top of his head. Where it wasn't covered by bristly black hair, Coach Kinen's skin was deeply tanned.

Danny's mom walked into the kitchen. "Danny? I was just telling Coach that you didn't even mention football practice." She stopped when she saw the coffee stains across the front of Coach's purple Crooked Creek football shirt.

"What happened here?" she demanded, looking at Danny.

"Nothing to worry about, Sharon," the coach said smoothly. "And I'm not mad at all, Danny. If you need some extra time after everything . . ." Coach Kinen put the hat back on his head. "Well, we all get that. It's just that you have to get your ten practices in before the first game. We open against Froston, and I know you won't want to miss that. . . ."

Danny looked at his feet, embarrassed.

"Okay, kiddo. We got our second session at five today, and tomorrow morning we go at seven thirty." Coach Kinen patted Danny's shoulder and reached for the door. Danny saw him motion to Danny's mom before slipping outside.

"I'll walk Coach to his truck," she said.

Danny washed up and made himself lunch. He was sitting at the table, halfway through the sandwich and a glass of milk, when his mom returned and sat down beside him. She reached over and took his free hand in hers. "Danny, Coach Kinen says he has someone he thinks you might like to talk to. Someone at the junior high."

"About what?"

"Just . . ." She waved a hand in the air before she asked, "Do you want to go to practice this afternoon?"

Danny shrugged, shook his head, and looked away. "I don't know," he mumbled.

"Coach said take this first day off." She nodded and picked up the coach's coffee cup, wiping where it had spilled. "Then start fresh tomorrow, right?"

Danny took another bite and chewed, licking a spot of ketchup from his lip. "I don't know."

"You don't know? You don't know *what*?"

Danny shrugged and stuffed the rest of the sandwich into his mouth. He got up and finished chewing on his way to the sink, where he drank down the last of his milk before rinsing the glass and his plate and heading for the door.

"Danny?"

He stopped. "Yes?" He held the door halfway open, but he was already out.

"Your father wanted you to play."

Danny winced and shut his eyes, squeezing back the tears. He turned and slammed the door and ran to the garage. He was breathing hard and he forced himself to count backward from one hundred by fives. He started up the mower, still counting, and set off down the driveway. Before he hit the road, he pulled on his headphones and turned up the playlist so that the sound was deafening. The vibration of the machine beneath his hands on the wheel was somehow soothing.

He was breathing normal again.

Without planning it, he stopped at Janey's house and rang the bell. Janey kept her long blonde hair pulled back in a pony-tail. She was nearly as tall as Danny, with big brown eyes, flecked with gold. Seeing her approach, Danny started to relax.

He told her what happened, and she nodded like she under-stood but got right to the point. "People probably would make less of a fuss if you didn't quit football."

"I didn't quit. I just . . . didn't start."

She looked at him and shrugged. "You know I don't care if you play. I'm just trying to help. Your mom's in a state. Cupcake called me and told me everyone's talking about Daniel Owens's son quitting football."

"Maybe everyone should mind their business."

"That'll be the day," she said. "Won't ever happen in this small town."

"Come on," Danny said. He climbed onto the John Deere and motioned his head for her to climb aboard. She nodded and sat facing the other way with her feet braced on the fenders. As he started the engine, he could feel the back of her head against his own and her shoulder blades cutting into his back. He liked the way that felt, rumbling down the shoulder of Route 222.

All too soon they came to the break in the guardrail before the bridge. Danny pulled over further onto the grass and cut the motor. He followed Janey down the bank and across the creek, finding footholds on rocks as familiar as his front steps. They climbed the far bank, grabbing a root halfway up that was worn smooth from acting as a handrail. They followed their own winding dirt path back to where the creek bowed and there were several small drops. They weren't waterfalls, but over thousands of years, the drop had created small slides of water, sluices that swirled into hollowed-out bathtubs of rock.

There were three rock tubs, one for each of them, within sight of their tree fort. Cupcake's was the biggest, twice as wide as Danny's, and Cupcake filled every inch of it. Janey stood beside it and chuckled. "Cupcake, I love that name. I love how he got it."

Almost everyone in Crooked Creek knew that story. Cupcake's real name was Eugene Wills. They were in third grade and just starting Pop Warner football. When Coach Hitchcock—a former marine—saw Eugene unsuccessfully try to defend himself against a blocker half his size, he went wild.

The coach stood over Eugene, who pawed the air like a turtle on its back.

"I never seen a cupcake big as you in my entire life!" Coach Hitchcock hollered so that everyone, including Danny's father and the other parents in the bleachers, heard him. "You gotta learn to *hit* someone, son, or you're never going to be able to play this game."

Back then, Eugene was a big blob of dough, and the name caught hold. The next day in school many of the kids jeered and called him Cupcake. The next night in practice, Eugene went berserk. Blubbery but intense, he steamrolled anyone who got in his way and then stood over their fallen bodies, red-faced and screaming, "That's right! I'm a cupcake! How's it feel to be crushed by a cupcake!"

Danny and Eugene had been friends even back then, and Danny was one of the few people who *hadn't* called him Cupcake. After Eugene had pummeled their quarterback, he bent down over the smaller player's crumpled form. "That's a *cup*cake for you! How'd you like *that* cupcake?"

Danny had tried to calm his friend, and he pulled him aside. "They're only kidding you, Eugene. Maybe lighten up."

His friend had turned to him with blazing eyes. "Don't call me Eugene. I'm Cupcake. Call me *Cupcake*."

Danny grinned, remembering how the legend was born.

"Come on," Janey said. "Let's go swimming." Janey stripped off her T-shirt and shorts, revealing a yellow bikini. She slid down into her own tub, the narrowest of the three, and laid her head back in the sluice so a fountain sprang up around her ponytail. "The water's nice and cool from the rain."

Danny stripped down to his boxers and lowered himself into his tub. The rock walls were smooth and soft with pale green algae. The water bubbled and swirled, and the sticky heat of the day was washed clean along with the grass clippings stuck to his legs.

Danny sighed and raised his voice above the babble of the water. "I could just stay here forever."

Janey giggled. "Me too."

After a time, he slid all the way down, slipping beneath the surface of the pool. Aside from the rush of swirling water, it was completely silent and dark. He turned thoughts over in his mind like smooth stones. He might have been the only person in the world, or an unborn baby in his mother's stomach, or on the other end of the journey, not the beginning, but the end . . . His dad had reached the end.

The sudden image of his father staring at him shocked Danny and plunged a dagger of pain into his heart.

Paralyzed by the memory, he just hung there, his arms and head suspended in the water, until he convulsed and exploded from the pool, gasping for air.

"Hey!" Janey shouted. She was standing in the middle of her tub, the water racing around her. "You scared me. What were you doing under there? Hey! Where you going?"

Danny waded through the water until he reached the bank. He pulled on his clothes as he sucked air into his lungs. "I gotta get back home and get some dinner and get some sleep."

"Why?" Janey asked as she sloshed across the creek. "What happened?"

Danny pulled the sweaty, grass-stained T-shirt over his

head and grinned at her. "I got football tomorrow."

She smiled. "That's great, Danny."

"Yeah, my dad wants me to . . . or, I mean, he *would* want me to." He looked down to concentrate on tying his sneaker. He sniffed and tied the other one, sensing Janey's presence right next to him. He stood and looked into her deep brown eyes.

She parted her lips, maybe to say something, but he was afraid she might try to kiss him, or that he might try to kiss her, and that scared him silent. He looked away to catch his breath before setting his mouth in a flat line and giving her a hardened look.

"I'm gonna do this for him," he said. "I'm dedicating this season to my dad."

The next day at practice it was clear to Danny that the eighth graders looked down on the seventh-grade players as youngsters who needed guidance and punishment. They were an intimidating bunch. One of the linemen, a big-bellied kid named Gabriel Stone, stood six feet tall and had to weigh north of 250. The kids called him Bug. In Danny's group of backs was a big, strong running back with long blond Viking hair and a mean face named John Markle. In each drill, the eighth grader raced to the front of the line. When Danny beat him to the gauntlet machine, Markle shoved him rudely out of the way and burst into and out of the machine before Danny could even react.

The gauntlet was essentially a cage with dozens of rigid padded arms connected to tight metal springs. If you didn't run full blast, the lower arms would trip you up and the upper arms would strip the ball from your hands. Danny recovered and went through it just as fast and easy as Markle had. The rest of the group struggled, but instead of sharing some camaraderie, Markle spit dangerously close to Danny's brand-new cleats as they stood in line. Danny burned inside and made sure that at every other drill they did, he outdid not only Markle but every other back, too. Two hours into practice, Danny made it known that he was faster, stronger, and tougher than any of the skill position players.

The real rub with Markle came when Coach Kinen called for the first-team offense to line up on the ball. Eighth-grade boys quickly filled in each of the eleven spots. Danny stood back with the other younger players, but Cupcake shoved the monster, Gabriel, out of his spot at right tackle before stepping in. "Hey!" Gabriel yelled as he wheeled around in disbelief. Fists quickly began to fly.

Coach Kinen and his assistant, Coach Willard, pulled the two of them apart, but the coaches seemed pleased.

"I like your spirit, Eugene."

"Call me Cupcake, Coach. That's my name." Cupcake didn't seem to mind snarling at his coach.

Coach Kinen chuckled. "Okay, Cupcake. That's funny. You play right guard and we'll leave Gabriel at right tackle."

"Okay." Cupcake nodded and shoved the kid at the right guard spot out of his way.

That kid looked at Coach Kinen with disbelief. "Coach, this kid is a seventh grader."

"And he's bigger, tougher, and stronger than you, Thomas. He starts until he proves he can't hold up." Coach Kinen turned toward the rest of the team as Thomas walked in shame away

34

from the starters. "This isn't a social club! Just because you *thought* you had a job doesn't mean you do. Coach Willard and I make those calls, and we do it to put the best team on the field so we can *win*!"

Coach Kinen stared around to see if anyone had anything to say about that before he shouted, "Markle! You're the backbone of our defense at middle linebacker. And you're the captain, you're the glue that holds your group together—if you can lead them. Can you do that, Markle?"

"Yes, Coach," he said sheepishly.

"Are you *sure*?"

"Yes, Coach," Markle yelled.

"Good. Good. And I want Danny Owens with the ones on offense at running back."

Markle looked like his head was ready to explode, but being named captain was a big deal, and he obviously knew better than to question Coach Kinen. But that didn't keep him from giving Danny a hateful look.

Danny ignored it. He was thrilled with the opportunity, and he intended to live up to Coach Kinen's faith in him.

Danny didn't disappoint Coach Kinen or anyone else over the next two weeks. He ran around people. He ran over them. He ran through them. By the time double sessions were over, most of his teammates—even the eighth graders—treated him with the respect that was reserved for a football team's star player, the one everyone knew would be the difference between winning and losing.

There were a couple of eighth graders, though, who either weren't convinced or, more likely, were too inflamed with jealousy to respect a seventh grader. It was the second-to-last practice before the first day of school when one of those boys made a very bad mistake.

Markle was rocking back and forth on his heels, clearly frustrated because now he was only starting on defense. On the last play of the team's live scrimmage period, Danny ran a sweep out around Markle's side.

The older boy tossed the tight end blocking him to the ground and took off at an angle to cut Danny off from the sideline. Danny poured on the speed, but he realized that he couldn't evade the older boy, who was also quite fast. Danny dipped his head inside with a shoulder fake to make Markle hesitate. Markle didn't buy it. He was willing to miss Danny entirely for the chance to hit him with every ounce of force he had. When the older boy launched himself at Danny, Danny jammed his hand, palm first, directly into Markle's facemask.

Markle went down like a slaughtered cow.

Danny churned his legs, so even though Markle was able to grab an ankle, Danny burst free without a pause and raced up the sideline into the end zone. Everyone had seen Danny's stiff-arm and Markle's disgrace, and they hooted and jeered and laughed out loud. It seemed like the teammates enjoyed it even more because of Markle's well-known bad feelings toward Danny.

Danny just blushed and smiled and jogged toward the sideline where Coach was having them line up for sprints. He fell in beside Cupcake when someone shoved him so hard he stumbled forward and toppled to the ground. Danny spun around to see Markle standing over him.

"You don't facemask your own team!" Markle's ugly face was red and pinched inside his helmet.

"Hey!" Cupcake bellowed, and charged the older boy.

Markle sidestepped Cupcake, threw a roundhouse punch into his gut, and shoved him into the dirt. Cupcake lay gasping for breath.

Danny was on his feet, and he opened his arms to diffuse the situation. "What's wrong with you? I didn't facemask you. That was a totally legal stiff-arm."

"That's bull." Markle leaned his face toward Danny's and jabbed a finger in his chest. "You cheat, maybe you get me, but you don't beat me legal."

"Whatever." Danny turned away. Most of the team hadn't seen the scuffle. They were lining up along the sideline and focused on surviving Coach Kinen's running program.

"Don't think you're so special!" Markle called after him. "Cuz you're not."

Danny helped Cupcake to his feet, ignoring the older boy.

"And neither was your old man," Markle sneered. "He was a freeloading fat-butt has-been."

Danny's vision blurred and went red. "Danny—" Cupcake reached for him, but Danny spun around and launched himself at Markle's throat. He grabbed his mask, twisted it, and yanked his teammate to the ground with a war cry. Danny gripped the mask with both hands and shook and twisted until it came free. He flung it aside. The helmet flew through the air, and before it hit the ground Danny was pummeling Markle's face.

Blowing his whistle, Coach Kinen came running and grabbed Danny by the shoulder pads. "Danny! Danny! Stop!"

Danny grabbed hold of Markle's jersey and shoulder pad. With his left hand clamped down on the padding, Danny continued to pound his teammate's face with his right hand. Even though Coach Kinen yanked Danny with all his might, he only dragged them both a few feet. Like a wasp, Danny had his adversary in a death grip and was stinging him repeatedly.

It took the two assistant coaches and Cupcake to finally pry Danny free. When they did, his mind cleared. He looked down at Markle and felt sick. The older boy's nose and cheeks were bloody and swollen. His eyes were two slits in the bruised fruit of his face. Markle was unrecognizable.

"What's wrong with you?" Coach Kinen screamed, staring and shaking his head. "What is *wrong* with you?"

Danny looked down at his swollen knuckles through teary eyes.

He had no idea what was wrong, only that he had lost his mind.

Crooked Creek rallied around its young football star. Word spread fast on social media and everyone agreed that John Markle had gotten what he was asking for, and certainly what he deserved. Janey and Cupcake kept Danny up to date, Janey by phone and Cupcake over the Xbox headset.

"Listen to this!"

"Cupcake, you're shouting." Danny turned down the headset volume.

"It's Jace Akers, bro. Jace Akers posted, 'Standing strong with my teammate Danny Owens, our seventh-grade stud RB. Respect.' Bro, he said 'respect.'"

"I know. You just read it." Danny sounded casual, but his grin stretched wide.

Jace Akers was an eighth grader, their quarterback, and the offensive team captain. Jace's girlfriend was a cheerleader and said to be the prettiest girl in the school. He'd always treated Danny nicely, but this was something different. At practice, the eighth graders still looked down on the seventh graders. Even guys like Danny and Cupcake, who were starters, got treated like unwanted relatives at best.

He made a mental note to thank Jace tomorrow at practice.

When it came time to shut down for the night, Danny briefly thought about Markle and his parents. Wait, parent. He was pretty sure Markle's father had moved away a long time ago. He pushed the thought of Markle's mom out of his head. What could she expect? With a kid like her son, she was probably used to fights and bloody noses.

He wandered out into the smoky living room. His mom had the TV on and a glass of strawberry vodka in her hand, which she nearly finished when she saw Danny.

"What's up, kiddo?" She sat on the couch with her legs curled underneath her.

"Just saying good night."

"So early?"

"Practice tomorrow is early. And then school starts the next day."

"Yeah, I knew that," she said, but he could tell by her expression that she hadn't known.

"Mom?"

"Yup?"

Danny paused because he didn't want this to come out wrong. "Maybe you should—I don't know—see if you can't find a job or something."

Her face softened. "You don't have to worry about money.

This house is paid for and your father's taken good care of us."

Danny couldn't keep his eyes off the glass in her hand. "It's not the money; I just thought you might like to have something to keep your mind off of things. With me going to school now is all I was thinking."

She smiled. "You're one sweet boy, Danny. You always were. Even when you were a baby. No crying. No fussing. You'd just lay there and smile and burp. For a while there I thought there was something wrong with you."

Danny knew she'd get mad if he said she was drinking too much. She always did when his dad said it. So instead he asked, "You okay?"

She waved him off. "Oh, I'm fine. As fine as I can be."

Danny stood silently for a moment before he said, "I got in a fight today at practice."

She grinned at him. "I heard all about it."

"Mrs. Markle called you?" Danny felt a twinge of concern.

"Sweetheart, I heard about it almost before it happened. His mother's keeping quiet, as she should. I'm proud of you. Everyone says he was asking for it." She raised her glass in a toast before taking the last sip. "That's the pride in you. You can't help who you are."

"Coach was mad."

"He'll get glad when you run through Froston at Thursday's game. It's Thursday, right?"

"Yes." He suddenly felt like he should hug his mom, but that made him uncomfortable. He'd grown up with his dad telling him not to be soft. Boys, his father said many a time, needed to be grabbed by the neck, not smothered with kisses and hugs. But Danny remembered now the hug his father had given him on the hill, before it happened. Maybe his father had been trying to tell him something?

The commercial on TV ended and his mom's show came back on, drawing her attention back to the screen. The moment passed, and Danny went to bed.

When Danny got to practice early the next morning, he walked over to where Jace was warming up his arm with Jake Moreland. Jake was Jace's best friend and the team's number one receiver.

"Hey, Jace."

"Hey, Danny." Jace fired the ball at Jake, who caught it with a soft thud.

"I just wanted to say thanks for that post."

"Yeah, well." Jace snatched Jake's return pass from the air. "Just don't bloody my nose, okay?"

They both laughed and it felt good to Danny to be standing there with the team captain, sharing a joke.

"You know what they say, right?" Jace asked.

"No. What?"

"Man's best friend is his dog, but a quarterback's best friend is his runner. So I got your back." Jace held the ball and flashed him a smile. "Even though you're a snot-nosed seventh grader."

They both laughed again and Danny felt his chest swell. He belonged there.

He felt good as he crawled beneath the sheets that night. He slept well and got up early, so he had plenty of time to comb his hair and check his appearance in the mirror. His mom liked to buy him nice things, dressing him up to look sharp in khakis and polo shirts.

Everyone knew everyone, but still, he was going to junior high, and there was some excitement in the air. He caught the bus and made room for Janey when she got on at her own stop. She wore a new dress, yellow with a white flower print. Her hair was the same, though. She wore no makeup and said she was grumpy because she'd slept poorly.

"What's up?" he asked.

"Nerves." She gave him a weak smile.

"I know, right? Junior high. All of a sudden we're not kids anymore."

"So they say." Janey brushed a loose strand of hair from her face and tucked it behind her ear. "I liked being a kid."

"You'll like this too. You look great." He offered an honest smile.

"To you."

"Hey, I'm a big deal. Just you wait till we play Froston. Sitting next to me will be worth something. You might have to get a ticket." He laughed at himself.

"Ticket? I'm on the team, buddy, and don't forget it."

"True, true."

They got off the bus and fell into the flow of students streaming across the circle, past its flagpole, and into the main entrance.

That's where they were waiting for him.

Coach Kinen was an eighth-grade math teacher, and he dressed the part with a short-sleeved shirt, a thin tie, and his bristly hair kind of uneven and dorky. The principal—Danny was pretty sure his name was Mr. Trufant—wore a light gray suit and brown suede shoes. His head was entirely bald and his steel-framed glasses gave him a villainous look. Then there was someone Danny didn't recognize, a thin man with a scruffy goatee wearing battered jeans and a plaid shirt open at the collar.

Mr. Trufant spoke first. "Danny? We need you to come with us."

Danny glanced at Janey. She looked shocked and even frightened.

When Danny hesitated, Coach Kinen took him by the arm. "It's going to be fine, Danny. We want to help."

Danny let his coach lead him away through the sea of gawking students with Mr. Trufant and the unknown man trailing behind. The four of them went into a conference room and the principal closed the door. He pointed to the long table. "Have a seat."

Danny and Coach Kinen sat on one side of the table. Taking a seat on the opposite side with the other man, Mr. Trufant said, "Danny, I want you to know that these two men are entirely on your side. As principal, I have to look at things from a wider viewpoint. So, where I see a serious assault on another student on school grounds, these two gentlemen see someone crying out for help."

"Hi, Danny," said the scruffy man, who looked young enough to be a student himself. "I'm Bob Crenshaw, the school counselor. It's nice to meet you."

Apparently that was all the counselor had to say. He folded his hands on the table and turned toward the principal.

Mr. Trufant cleared his throat. "You had a study hall third period, but I switched your schedule so that you now have your study hall first period. For now, you'll report to Mr. Crenshaw for that study hall. He'll determine which days you go to the library and which days you'll be spending first period with him."

Despite the serious looks on the three men's faces, Danny chuckled and looked the principal in the eye, offering a humble but charming smile, just like he'd been taught. "I'm not sure what this is about, sir. I'm fine. Markle insulted my family— my dad, actually—and we got into it. That's all."

Danny looked at his coach. His lips were squeezed together

tight, eyes glued to the principal, giving Danny no hope of rescue.

"That's not all, Danny." Mr. Trufant had a folder Danny hadn't noticed. He laid it on the table and removed a color copy of a photo. It showed John Markle's battered face. Aside from the long blond hair, and knowing that he had taken a beating yesterday, Danny would not have recognized the boy. He shifted uncomfortably in his seat.

The principal glared at Coach Kinen as if he'd done something wrong. "Do I need to spell this out, Dave?"

"No." Coach Kinen shook his head.

"Did you contact the mother?" asked the principal.

"She didn't answer, but I left a message and I'm sure she'll call me back." The coach turned to Danny. "Look, Danny, this is serious. You need to trust me and go along with whatever Mr. Trufant says. He is our friend in all this. You understand?"

"I'm not sure."

"Okay," said his coach, taking a deep breath. "I'll spell it out. There are people, including Markle's mom, who would like to see you suspended from school and banned from the football team for the entire season."

Danny swallowed and nodded that he understood. "But he started it."

Coach Kinen banged his palm on the table and everyone jumped. "That's irrelevant. Get that through your head. You need to get in line here. Or you definitely won't be playing football. And we need you to play ball. The team needs you."

"Okay." Danny kept his chin up.

"Is your mom at work or something? She's not away, is she?" the coach asked.

Danny thought about last night's strawberry vodkas. "She's probably asleep. She wasn't feeling well."

"Make sure she gives me a call." The coach looked at the principal, who nodded with approval. "You're gonna like Mr. Crenshaw. He's going to help you, Danny—and you're not going to fight us on this, are you?"

"No, sir."

"See?" Coach Kinen said to the other two men. "This'll all work out. Danny, you go with Mr. Crenshaw, and I'll see you at practice."

"Good, then." The principal patted the table like it was a horse's rump, stood, and went off to begin the announcements.

Coach Kinen gave Danny's shoulder a squeeze, and then he left.

Crenshaw sat looking at Danny with a curious smile.

Danny couldn't help frowning back at him and asking, "So, what now?"

Crenshaw had blue eyes and a short haircut styled with gel. He stroked his goatee, which was no more than the thin beginnings of a bird nest. "Now we get to know each other."

"You're not gonna make me lay down on a couch and have me tell you about my mother?" Danny had seen shrinks on TV.

Crenshaw's face became serious. "Do you want to tell me anything about your mother?"

"No."

"Fine." Crenshaw leaned toward him. "Is there *anything* you'd like to tell me?"

Danny snorted softly. "I'm fine, so . . ."

Danny made a zero with his thumb and forefinger and looked through the hole at the counselor.

Crenshaw was unfazed by Danny's refusal. He leaned back and sat watching and smiling. Danny put down his zero and smiled back until he got annoyed. "This is what you do? You sit and stare?"

"I'm happy to do whatever you'd like to do. This is your time. Would you like to go to my office?"

"Why?"

Crenshaw shrugged and looked around. "It's a little less sterile. I've got some games."

"Games?" Danny wrinkled his face. "What, like Chutes and Ladders? Hungry Hungry Hippos?"

"No, but I could get those if that's what you want." Crenshaw said it with a straight face.

"I bloodied someone's face," Danny said, wanting to provoke him. "You think I play baby games?"

"I prefer Rummikub or Yahtzee, but I'm happy to do whatever."

"Great." Danny stood up. "Whatever is I go to the library and you play . . . What'd you say? Rummy Cube? Or Kamikaze? Whatever floats your boat. Sound good?"

Crenshaw stood up too. He walked past Danny and opened the door as the principal began the announcements. "Come on. We'll go to my office."

"I thought you said 'whatever'?" Danny followed him into the hall, feeling free already.

"Whatever, together." They didn't go far before Crenshaw used a key to open a faded wooden door with no lettering. "Come on in."

Crenshaw's office was cool from the AC. It had one shaded window and a fish tank on top of the bookshelf. Along one wall was that couch Danny expected, but in the corner opposite

Crenshaw's desk was a table with two chairs. A plastic chess set showed a game at its midpoint. On the shelves beside it were other games Danny didn't recognize. Board games were for kids. "No Xbox?"

Crenshaw took the chair behind his desk and put up his feet. "No electronics. School rules, not mine."

"Otherwise you'd have, what? A computer chess game?" It bothered Danny that the school counselor was so calm and comfortable. "Some lame TV show? *Family Feud*?"

"Nah, I'm an Xbox guy. *Assassin's Creed*, some *NBA2K*. *Halo* if I'm on with my brother. He lives in Seattle." Crenshaw pointed at the shelves. "But here it's all chess and Rummikub."

Danny flopped down on the couch. "No thanks. I'll just sit."

"You can read." Crenshaw pointed at the books.

Danny laughed out loud.

"No?" Crenshaw looked at him sharply. "That's not something you do?"

Danny felt his spine stiffen.

"We could talk," Crenshaw said.

Danny scowled. "I'll read."

"Have at it." Crenshaw held out an open palm toward the books.

Danny saw a purple cover. He pulled it out. A knight on horseback with his sword drawn surveyed a distant castle where a dragon sailed among the clouds. Danny opened the book, studying the words.

Crenshaw sighed and took out a book of his own.

Every so often, Danny would turn a page. In between he thought about what happened to Markle, how it was just a fight, how he felt fine and didn't get the big deal. He thought first period would never end.

Finally the bell rang and Danny scrambled for the door.

"You'll need to check into the office to get your locker." Crenshaw lowered his book, but otherwise sat unmoving behind the desk. "And I'll see you tomorrow."

Danny broke free and put distance between him and the counselor's office because no way did he want people thinking he was a mental case. His teeth were clenched and he hammered a random locker with the soft part of his fist. It produced a satisfying crash, drawing stares from students entering the hallway. Danny warned them with a glare. He knew how quickly word of his thrashing Markle had spread. It would get out even quicker about Crenshaw.

He stomped toward the main office. He'd get his locker, dump his stuff, then find Janey as soon as he could. Janey was smart. She was clever. She'd know how to help him, because he was pretty determined that he was not going back to Crenshaw's.

Even if it meant doing something extreme.

"You can't run away." Janey stood with Danny in the hallway as a sea of kids foamed around them. "Your team needs you. Your *mom* needs you."

"But I can't do Crenshaw," Danny said, shifting his eyes. "Everyone will think I'm a nutter."

"Stop." She shooed away the idea with the back of her hand. "People go to counseling all the time. Smart people. You should at least talk to him."

Danny huffed. He didn't like when Janey had her mind made up. She'd never change now.

"Speaking of smart, do you have Ms. Rait third period for English?" he asked.

"I do." She removed the schedule from her bag and they compared classes. They were together for English, history, lunch, and gym.

"I heard she's got a crutch."

Janey shrugged. "So."

Danny shrugged. "I don't know. It's different."

"I like different." She bumped him with her shoulder. "That's why I like you."

"I'm not so different," Danny muttered, but his chest swelled with pride.

Her face turned serious. "Talk to the counselor. It might be good. No one will think anything. Everyone knows about your dad, and the fight."

"You think they know Mr. Trufant is making me do this?"

"Yes, but maybe it will help."

"Help what?" Danny felt his nostrils flare. "I don't *need* any stupid help."

"Danny," she said softly. She studied him with a sad look. Then the first bell rang and she looked toward the tall ceiling of the grand old school that had been built nearly a hundred years ago. "Okay, see you in English."

Danny had math with Cupcake. Danny liked math. When it was just numbers, he crushed math, and it made him feel smart. Their teacher, Mr. Doan, was a scarecrow with thick eyebrows and glasses. He was squeaking his marker on the board like a hungry baby bird when Cupcake ripped through the silence with a fart.

A few random titters were quickly gulped back, not because Mr. Doan froze at the board, but because no one was going to dare laugh at Cupcake. Cupcake's big round face turned bright red, but only Danny would even look at him, and Danny's shrug and the look on his face said, *Things happen.*

Mr. Doan must have seen Danny because he had turned around and he now said, "Mr. Owens, do you need to use the bathroom?"

That got everyone laughing, even Cupcake, especially when Danny went along with a straight face. "No, sir."

That sent people off their seats because the students all knew it was Cupcake's bomb. Mr. Doan sniffed the air. "Good night!"

The teacher scrambled for the window and flung it open so he could breathe. Danny sat like a scolded angel, staring straight ahead and biting his cheek to avoid grinning amid the roar of laughter.

Things finally settled down and Mr. Doan got back to the board. When he asked Danny to come up and demonstrate the division of fractions he'd been teaching, it seemed like a punishment, but Danny turned it into a show by jotting the answers on the board as fast as Mr. Doan could write the numbers. When the bell rang, Danny wasn't surprised to hear the teacher call his name.

Cupcake gave Danny a look of apology on his way out the door. Danny stood at attention beside the teacher's desk.

Mr. Doan pushed the glasses up on his nose. "You know your math, Mr. Owens; now, if we can get you to exhibit the same proficiency with your manners, you and I might have a fine time this year."

"I'm sorry, Mr. Doan, but it wasn't me," Danny said, flashing a smile. "I just didn't want to rat someone out."

"Ahh . . . I see." Mr. Doan stared at Danny, looking for the truth and finding it. "Well, do me a favor then and tell whoever did do it to excuse themselves to the bathroom next time so I don't have to make a federal case of it."

"I will, sir." The first bell rang and kids began streaming into the class from the hallway. Danny looked up at the sound. "Can I go?"

"Yes, of course. And that was a good job at the board, Mr. Owens."

Danny hurried to English class. It was on the opposite side of the school. He was three doors down when the second bell rang. He took off and nearly knocked over the teacher as he hustled through the door. She staggered sideways and caught herself with the metal crutch fastened to her left arm.

"I'm . . . oh my gosh, I'm sorry." Danny couldn't keep his eyes from drinking in the teacher's crooked leg in her skintight jeans. When he met her eyes, they were aflame.

Ms. Rait was dark haired and pretty, with big dark brown eyes. Her shoulders were square and strong beneath a black silk blouse.

"You're late, Mr. . . . ?"

"Owens, ma'am, Danny Owens."

"Sit down, Mr. Owens."

"Yes, ma'am."

The teacher turned her back on him and delivered the rest of her papers to Janey, who sat in the last seat of the front row. Janey had saved the seat behind her for Danny. He slipped into the desk, took a stapled group of papers from Janey, and passed the rest back.

Ms. Rait stood beside her desk now with her back as straight as her leg was crooked. "There are fifty questions, multiple choice. You have twenty minutes to answer them."

Danny's hand went up. "Wait. What?"

"A pretest, Mr. Owens." Ms. Rait spoke with the authority of a football coach. "To glean what you know and don't know. You'd know that if you'd been on time, but we can talk more after school . . ."

"After?"

"Yes, in detention for being late. We have a lot of material to cover this year and being late won't get it done." The teacher scowled at her wristwatch. "Ready? Go."

Danny sat blinking at her, but she paid him no mind. Instead, she took a seat at her desk and opened a book.

Danny swallowed the lump in his throat and glanced around. He had that awful twist in his gut as he looked down at the page. The room was silent, with twenty-six kids bent over their desks, quickly circling their answers.

Danny took a deep breath and gently poked Janey's back with his pencil. He sighed with relief as she pushed her test to the upper left corner of her desk where he could clearly see the answers.

His eyes worked like little rodents, scurrying here and there for morsels of information, but never stopping to rest and always checking to see that Ms. Rait was well occupied by her book.

It wasn't until the final two answers, both B, when Danny looked up and saw Ms. Rait staring directly at him.

Danny looked away.

He furrowed his brow and pretended to be grinding on his test. When he tried to sneak a peek at the teacher she was still staring, unmoved. Danny had that sinking feeling in his gut. He circled B for the next answer and then D for the last answer to throw her off.

It seemed like forever before Ms. Rait called, "Time."

She struggled up from her desk without expression. "Please pass your tests to the front."

Secretly, Danny watched her collecting the tests. When she took the stack from Janey, she paid him no mind, and he thought maybe the whole thing was going to blow over. He felt like that was pretty decent of her—to give him a break on the first day even though she'd given him detention for being late. He understood that. It was like a football coach. Ms. Rait was making him an example so everyone knew she was serious, but when it came to something only she and he knew about, well, she let that slide.

When she began to lecture them on the importance of reading, Danny felt his eyelids sagging. He opened his notebook and drew up some football plays to make it look like he was with the program. Ms. Rait illustrated charts for them on the board that sketched out plotlines, story arcs, and what she called "essential characters," but her point was that reading was supposed to be fun. Danny snorted softly at that one.

When Ms. Rait turned back to face her class, excitement glowed in her eyes. "And while we will learn the elements of stories and writing and work to shore up your mechanics—spelling, punctuation, grammar—my focus will be for you to read, read, read, and read some more. It should be fun. It should be exciting. It should be life changing."

She looked around like a woman waking from a dream.

Danny forgot about his troubles and actually felt bad for her because she was pretty and nice and she had that crutch thing going.

From the middle of the classroom, Pete Goff raised his hand. Pete had also made the team as a seventh grader, not as a starter like Cupcake and Danny, though. He was a second-string offensive tackle. While he didn't have Cupcake's size, Pete was also a farm kid and had all the toughness and strength that went with that.

"Yes, Mr. . . . Goff, is it?"

"Yes, ma'am. Ma'am, do you like football?"

A small wave of tittering rolled through the classroom.

"Why would you ask me that, Mr. Goff?"

Pete scratched at the red stubble on his scalp. "Well, you said fun and exciting and life changing. Sounds like you're talkin' football. These parts that's how it goes anyways."

Ms. Rait was obviously disappointed that Pete wasn't drinking her Kool-Aid, but she forced a smile. "I understand the attraction to football, and all sports, but this is something vastly more important. Reading is the cornerstone of education, and education is how we better ourselves as individuals and a society."

She looked around at them to show she was serious, and the bell rang.

Ms. Rait raised her voice above the scramble. "There are copies of *Bud, Not Buddy* on the desk by the door! Take one and read chapter one for tomorrow! There may be a quiz!"

As the groans subsided, Ms. Rait spoke in a lower but clear voice. "Mr. Owens, I need to see you."

"Yes, ma'am."

Janey turned toward him and bit her lip. Her eyes filled with panic, maybe for him, but maybe for her too. Janey was always at the top of their class, and trouble was something she avoided like it was a raccoon with rabies. He knew she didn't like when he looked at her answers, but they both knew English killed him and without her he'd likely not have made it past third grade. To calm her, Danny held his chin high and gave his head a slight shake to signal that he'd never take her down too.

When Janey turned and disappeared into the hall, Danny turned to face the music.

"Close that door," his teacher said.

"Yes, ma'am."

Danny did as told and approached the desk where she now sat with one arm still connected to the crutch. He noticed now a little fuzzy purple koala bear clipped to the aluminum support and wondered where it came from.

"I'm sorry we have to start out this way, but cheating is a very serious thing with me." Her eyes flashed with anger.

"I—"

She held up a hand. "Lying is even worse, so think about what you want to say to me before you say it."

Danny smiled nervously and forced a laugh. "Number fifty was just so hard, and I saw Janey's paper and I did look, but I didn't even use her answer. I swear. You can check."

Danny pointed to the stack of tests.

Ms. Rait stretched her lips with doubt. Then she breathed in through her nose before letting it out in a huff. She reached for the tests, rifled through the pile, and removed his and Janey's. She put them down and flipped to the last page.

Danny bit back a smile, well pleased with his own cleverness, until she frowned and began working backwards to compare the other answers.

"These are all the same," she said without looking up. "The rest of them."

"Really?" Danny craned his neck, wearing a mask of incredible surprise.

She snapped the papers down and glared up at him. "Very clever. You saw me see you and you changed it."

"No, ma'am." Danny swapped his smiling face for a look of horror. "Ms. Rait, why don't you like me? Is this just cuz I was late? My math teacher kept me and that class is on the other side of the school."

She studied him and crimped her lips. "You're very charming, Danny, with your 'yes, ma'am,' 'no, ma'am,' but I see through charm."

She raised her crutch just off the floor. "Outward appearances don't mean as much to me. I'm interested about the inside."

"Ma'am . . ." Danny sighed. "I's just being polite."

"I *was* just being polite," she said, correcting him.

"Was."

Someone for her next class knocked gently on the door and

peered through the window.

"Well, it's your word against mine. I can't prove you cheated." She smiled at him in a way that suggested she'd won a contest. "But I've got a better idea. I'll have you retake the test after school.

"See you then, Danny."

After health class, Danny found Cupcake and Janey in the cafeteria. Cupcake had his four sandwiches laid out in the order he planned to eat them. Today, he was starting with ham and ending with a PB&J. Janey munched on a carrot stick.

Cupcake took a huge bite and spoke through his food. "Well, beef or barley?"

Cupcake liked to break everything down into beef—something valuable and delicious—or barley—something mushy and inedible unless you were a cow.

"Barley." Danny slumped down in the chair next to Janey and removed a leftover chicken leg from his paper sack. "She's making me take the test again, after school."

"Hm." Cupcake raised his eyebrows. "I thought she was pretty beefy."

"She's not beefy." Janey scowled at him. "She's pretty."

"That's what I said." Cupcake gave her an annoyed look. "Beef is good. She looks good—pretty to you, beefy to me." Janey shook her head, then looked at Danny. "Ms. Rait didn't think I was in on it, did she?"

"If she did, she didn't say." Danny saw that wasn't quite what she wanted to hear, so he added, "She would have said if she did. I told her I looked at your paper but put down my own answer."

"But she'll just check."

"Yeah. She did, and she saw I *did* have a different answer, so she can't prove anything." Danny gave her a knowing look.

She high-fived him. "Genius."

"Except now she wants me to take the test on my own after school." Danny lowered his head and gently bumped it against the lunch table. "I'm dead."

Cupcake said, "Bro, you're a C student. What's the worry?"

"I pray for Cs in English," Danny said.

Cupcake nodded. "Okay, but you score Bs in math. You can handle it. My brother always says, 'C is for degree.' Get it? You get Cs, you graduate. You're gonna be a five-star recruit. You don't have to get all As like Miss Fancy Pants here."

"D is for degree," Janey said rolling her eyes. "And why do straight As make me fancy?"

"Not the letter 'C,'" Cupcake said impatiently, filling his mouth again. "The grade. So much for straight As being a smart marker."

"Forget it." Janey gave her carrot a final crunch and sighed. "Danny, I wish you hadn't poked me."

He shrugged. "I panicked. I don't want her thinking I'm stupid."

Janey frowned. "What about Coach Kinen? Can't *he* help you get out of it? I mean, you didn't have all the same answers as me—she told you herself she couldn't prove it—and isn't that what football coaches do?"

"I heard Coach Oglethorpe was the one who kept those three varsity linemen out of jail last year after they spray-painted all those cars in East Mormont," Cupcake said.

"I'm not going to jail." Danny waved his hand like he was swatting away trouble. "We're talking about an English test."

"Yeah, but we're also talking about the magical powers of football coaches in Texas, right?" A bit of crust escaped Cupcake's jaws.

"Shouldn't you try?" Janey asked. "They all know you've had a rough summer. Maybe she'll cut you a break if Coach Kinen asks her to."

"Naw." Danny poked his oatmeal cookie, leaving a dimple. "I'll save it for when I really need it. You're right. It's a pretest. So I flop. What can she do to me, right?"

Cupcake's lower lip slipped under his teeth and his eyebrows jumped. "With teachers, bro? That is one question you never want to ask, cuz they can always do something. Trust me on that."

At three o'clock, Danny pushed through the hallways filled with students running to catch buses home. He walked into Ms. Rait's classroom with his head high. He was ready to take whatever medicine she dished out. He'd flop on this test, choke it down, and move on.

She was reading a book, and he wondered if that was for real or if she was just doing it for his benefit.

"Ah, Mr. Owens." She thumped the book shut and set it down before getting up and pointing to the desk closest to hers. "Sit right down."

Danny sat and accepted the test she handed him. He counted each thump her crutch made against the floor as she returned to her seat, eight in all.

"Okay," she said, taking out her phone and bringing up a screen he assumed was a timer. "Ready? Go."

Danny bent his head over the test, all business, but it was playacting for him. He put on the face of a general studying his battlefield map. He knew how to get by. You "yes, ma'amed" and "no, ma'amed" till you were blue in the face. You turned on that toothy smile. You spoke softly and asked for a little extra help and with it came that little extra consideration so that an F might become a D or even a C and you'd get by.

Janey helped with the homework, and she'd never hide her test paper from his sight like some kids did.

Seeing that Ms. Rait had her nose back in her book, Danny's eyes drifted toward the tall narrow glass of the old window. The hardware had been painted over and the paint was dusty and cracked. A thick beam of sunlight muscled its way into the classroom. Dust danced in a wild swirl. Danny heard the shouts of kids somewhere outside, sounds of freedom.

He sighed and looked at the test and began to circle random answers, forcing himself to go slow in case she snuck a peek at him. It took forever, but finally she called out, "Time."

Danny made a show of quickly circling the last answer, and to save her the effort, he popped up from his chair and delivered the test to her desk. Smiling—but not too much—he said, "Okay, ma'am. See you tomorrow."

"Mr. Owens, what about me don't you understand?"

"Ma'am?"

She pointed toward the desk he'd just left. "I say what I mean and I mean what I say. Detention. You need to sit for twenty more minutes before you're off to football. You play football, correct?"

Danny sat back down and, just as he'd been doing since

kindergarten, politely folded his hands, because he needed to get on this teacher's good side. "Yes, ma'am. I'm the halfback."

"Ah, half of a fullback but two times a quarterback."

Danny laughed just the right amount at her joke. "Well, a halfback runs the ball downfield about half of all the plays. And I try to run it into the end zone each and every time."

"I can't say I knew that," she said thoughtfully, "but I have the feeling I'm going to learn around here."

"Yes, ma'am. Football is king in Texas. Everybody goes to the games. Even the junior high ones." Danny paused, then said, "Ma'am? What made you come to Crooked Creek?"

"A job," she said, and he could feel her softening toward him. "Oh, I have an aunt in Jericho, but we're not all that close. Also, I grew up in Chicago and I always told myself I'd live in a small town."

"Small towns are like family, you know?" This was going better than expected. "Everyone kinda watching out for each other."

"Like sharing test answers?" she said, ruining his smile. "Let's see how you did on your own, shall we?"

He watched her eyes as she began to grade his test. He watched the color deepen in her face and her mouth become a slit so tight it might have been a paper cut.

She looked up. "Is this some kind of a joke, Mr. Owens?"

"No, ma'am." He studied his hands.

"Stop with the 'ma'am.' I'm not your ma'am. I want to know what this is about." She picked his test up off her desk like it was someone's used Kleenex. "You scored a twenty-eight."

He glanced up, then put his head back down. "I'm not very good at English, M-Ms. Rait."

"Did you do this intentionally?" She waved the test.

"Last year, Mrs. Morgan—my sixth-grade English teacher—she'd let me do corrections on my tests and then take the average of the two. That way I could really learn it all, and pass, too." Danny looked up, hopeful that they could come to a similar arrangement.

"And you'd take these tests home to redo them?" Ms. Rait asked.

"Yes," he said, excited that she was getting this.

"And someone would help you? Like tutor you, a kind of coach? Maybe that girl, Janey?"

"She's my best friend and the smartest person in the world, so, yeah, she works with me some." He studied his teacher's eyes, but he couldn't read them.

She watched him and he knew she was turning things over in her mind. Finally, she got up and thumped over to the board. She steadied herself and, after a great deal of squeaking, produced a word.

She spun her head around at him. "What is this word?"

Danny's face burned. He forced a laugh. "I'm not good at this, Ms. Rait. I get nervous. I don't know why."

She screeched out another word with her marker, this time shorter, just four letters. Danny's mouth opened and closed like a fish in the bottom of a boat. She wrote two letters.

"Toe!" he said.

She frowned and pointed at the letters on the whiteboard

with her marker, leaving little smudges beside them. "T-O. It spells 'to,' Danny. Very close. Do you have any idea what this one is?"

She made a smudge beneath the letters H-O-M-E.

He tried to decipher it, but he knew he'd be wrong. He crossed his arms to hold himself in and said nothing.

"Danny?" Ms. Rait spoke in a voice soft as a cloud. "Danny, you can't read, can you?"

Danny burst out of his seat and made for the door. No way was she stopping him.

"I can read!" He spit his words before slamming the door behind him and heading for football practice.

The locker room was in mayhem. Hoots, hollers, and laughter zinged back and forth through the air, ricocheting off the metal lockers like bullets. It was the perfect place to get lost in. Danny opened his locker and angrily dug into the stuffing of equipment and clothes.

He layered on the pads and wiggled into his jersey. When his head popped through, there was Cupcake.

"How was it, bro? Detention?"

Danny pushed past him and mumbled, "I don't want to talk about it."

His cleats clapped the floor. He slammed open the metal

exit door, escaping into the afternoon sun. Sweat jumped from his skin. He breathed in the heat and kept going. The green grass of the practice field was an oasis—not a shady place to escape the heat, but to escape the crazy burning in his brain. It was like his entire life was coming unwound, but out there, between the lines, he'd be free from all that.

He went right to the single blocking sled, got in a stance, and fired out, striking it with all his might and launching it over the hot grass. Cupcake came and stood and watched until it became clear that Danny wasn't talking, and he walked away.

Danny was still working the sled when Coach Kinen blew the whistle.

The team stretched and warmed up, doing agility drills before breaking down into smaller groups based on positions. Coach Kinen took the skill positions—quarterbacks, running backs, and wide receivers. Coach Willard, a big, crusty old lineman himself, took the linemen.

Danny had no issues—in fact, Coach Kinen praised him several times for his intensity—until the last part of practice. Coach called a forty-eight toss sweep. Jace took the snap, turned, and tossed the ball on an easy curve out into the space in front of Danny. Danny caught the ball and took off.

The play-side wide receiver, Duval Carmody, blocked his defender in, giving Danny the corner and a free run up the sideline. From the inside of the defense, the middle linebacker was heading his way, unblocked. All Danny had to do was outrun him, but he didn't.

Danny planted a foot in the ground and cut back so he could meet the middle linebacker with a full head of steam.

Their pads cracked. Danny plowed up through the defender, knocking him flat on his back, while the churn of Danny's own feet kept him going forward. He ran over the linebacker, but the linebacker held on to his jersey, slowing Danny so that two lumbering linemen could get there and bring him down after a nine-yard gain.

Danny sprang to his feet, growling and pumping a fist in the air. "Yes! Yes! Yes!"

Cupcake arrived at the scene and roared. "Pancake run! Yes! You flattened him."

They bumped chests and slapped high fives all the way back to the huddle.

Coach Kinen stood with his eyes hidden behind aviator sunglasses beneath the bill of his cap. "Danny? What the heck was that?"

Danny laughed. "I pancaked him, Coach."

Coach Kinen wasn't laughing. He wasn't even smiling. "You had the outside. Carmody had the cornerback pinned. That was a touchdown that you just turned into a nine-yard run."

Danny scowled and sunk his teeth into the rubber mouth guard that slurred his speech.

"Let's go!" Coach Kinen shouted at his offense. "Get in the huddle!"

The next play, Danny was supposed to go in motion and run a corner route, but he ran a post and laid out the free safety. After that, he missed his blocking assignment on a pass play, allowing the inside linebacker a free shot at Jace, even though he did punish the outside linebacker with a smashing block.

And so it went. Danny's practice became a series of mistakes and mishaps, each one sending his mind further and further off course. After sprints and a pep talk, Coach Kinen turned his team loose before calling Danny back.

Danny stood huffing and sweating while his coach seemed to study him. Finally, Coach Kinen said, "Danny, we open the season in three days and I gotta know where your head is at."

Danny looked away. Some heavy white clouds, stacked miles high, advanced on Crooked Creek like an armada of tall ships.

"Danny? Are you with me? Did something happen?"

Danny bit his lip to keep from getting emotional. "My English teacher hates me. I have no idea why; I think it's a football thing. I don't know . . ."

"Rait?" Coach looked like he had tasted a lemon.

"Yeah." Danny explained everything that had happened, leaving out the part about her accusing him of not being able to read. "I'm terrible in English, Coach. Last year Mrs. Morgan helped me out. With this lady, I don't know what's gonna happen."

Coach Kinen frowned. "Well, let me see what I can do. We can't have her failing you. The marking period ends the week before the championship. It'd be a crime if you couldn't play in the big game just because we've got some new teacher who doesn't know what's what. You let me work on this. Just make sure you do that Crenshaw thing—see him every day—without any trouble, okay?"

"Sure," Danny said. "He's okay."

"Good. Okay, get out of here."

Danny felt instantly better. The heat didn't seem so hot

and the sweat stopped stinging his eyes. He changed in the locker room. When he slammed his locker shut, he turned and bumped into Bug, the huge offensive lineman who played right tackle next to Cupcake. Bug still had his football pants on beneath his big naked belly.

"Hey." It was more of a grunt than a greeting. "I liked that pancake you had." Gabriel scratched his belly. "Making a bonfire Saturday night. You can come."

Danny didn't know what to say, but it didn't matter. The enormous lineman was walking away.

"Thanks," Danny said.

He headed outside with Cupcake, telling him about the invite as they went.

Cupcake stopped and took Danny by the arm. "Bro, he's called 'Bug' for a reason. He's as weird as a three-dollar bill, but man can he drive block."

"Why 'Bug'?"

"Like Firebug. He never saw a pack of matches he didn't want to light. He does these bonfires in the woods behind the old concrete factory just outside of town. Works on them all week, stacking branches and wood as high as he can."

"Lots of kids make bonfires," Danny said.

"Yeah, or light brush piles or old sheds and stuff; I know. We live in the country. But they say when Bug lights his fires, he just stares at the flames. Doesn't say a word, but his lips move."

"Now, that's weird."

"Yup."

They kept going to the parking lot where Cupcake's brother,

Herman, picked them up in a dirt-covered pickup. There was a sports bus that took kids home after practices let out, but it took so long to bring Cupcake home that his dad sent his older brother to get him so he could make an early dinner before helping with evening chores on the farm. Herman took after Cupcake's dad, skinny as a beanpole with a beard wider than his hips. Cupcake was like his mom's side, big boned and built like a barn. Danny's house was right on the way to Cupcake's place, and Herman was always happy to drop him off.

Danny got out in his driveway and waved at Cupcake as they drove away in a cloud of dust. He smelled liver the instant he opened the door. His mom stood over a frying pan with a cigarette in one hand and a spatula in the other. The air was warm and heavy even though the AC was on full blast.

"Pour us some iced tea." By her tone, Danny could tell there was something she wanted to say. "Dinner's almost ready."

The plates and silverware had been laid out. There were three places. Danny didn't want to ask if they were having company or if she'd just forgotten his father was gone. She'd done it before. He scooped some ice and filled two glasses. If a guest was coming she'd say so now, but she didn't.

Danny sat and waited until she carried the fry pan over to the table and unloaded the liver and bacon and onions onto their plates in a swirl of steam. They rarely ate liver. Danny and his mom loved it, but his dad hadn't cared for it much and it usually caused a fight.

Danny held his knife and fork, but he paused before eating. "You wanting to say something?"

"Put your napkin in your lap," she said, showing him how like he'd never done so before. "Eat your supper, then we can talk."

Danny hesitated, realizing two things: First, his mother had that mulish look on her face that said she would not be changing her mind. Second, the smell of the food was making his mouth water.

"Okay," he said.

She butted out her smoke in the ashtray and picked at her food. Danny cleaned his plate in short order before pushing it away from him and leaning back.

"So?" He eyed her cautiously.

"So." She pulled the garbage can out from under the sink so he could see it.

Then she headed to the fridge.

He watched her take a half-empty vodka bottle out of the freezer and pour it down the drain. Then she reached behind a stack of frozen vegetables and pulled out another bottle.

She emptied that, too.

Looking at him, she lifted each bottle ceremoniously and dropped it in the garbage.

"What are you doing?" he asked.

"What are *we* doing, you mean," she said. "We are taking control of our lives."

"So why don't you throw out the cigarettes, too?"

"Danny, you gotta work on one vice, one day at a time. They're next, though."

She tied up the garbage bag and carried it to the back door, tossing it with a crash before returning to sit. "I got a call from Coach Kinen."

Danny nodded.

"He told me about the counselor, and about the issue with your teacher." She tilted her head. "You're making your mark, I'd say, but not the way I'd like you to be."

"Mom—"

She held up a hand to stop him, but he wanted to explain how the whole thing was nonsense. Markle got what he deserved and his teacher was a crab who Coach Kinen would set straight.

"No. Listen. This is my fault as much as yours," she said. "I need to get better, and you need to get better, and that's what we're going to do. No more smoking. No more drinking. No more fighting. And no more cheating."

She paused dramatically and delivered a bombshell.

"Danny, the teacher thinks you can't read."

Danny's face heated up and he looked at his plate.

"You're a smart boy, Danny." His mother sweetened her voice with kindness. "You can do your own work. You don't have to be like Janey. Not many people are. Just be you. Maybe a little more studying and a little less Xbox, okay?"

"Sure."

He needed to get out of Rait's class, and he hoped Coach Kinen could make it happen. He'd already heard that the other seventh-grade English teacher was a pushover. She was ancient, old enough to be a grandmother. She wore thick glasses and had hearing aids that needed constant adjustment.

"I think Coach Kinen is going to get me into a different English class and everything will be fine."

"Okay, but no copying on tests, right?"

"Okay," he said, wanting to believe he meant it.

"And this Mr. Crenshaw, let's give him a chance. He seems nice, and he likes you, Danny."

"You spoke to him?"

"Yes. I wanted to know what it was all about, and I'm glad they're trying to help you. After your father—" She paused before continuing. "Well, I know you must be feeling things. Look, everyone's on your side, Danny. Especially me, even though I haven't showed it. We're going to see the principal tomorrow. And we'll show them we're okay."

"Mom—"

"Don't argue. We're going." She sighed deeply and looked around. "So let's clean up the kitchen and go to town for some ice cream. You can ask your girlfriend."

"Janey is not my girlfriend, Mom." Danny didn't know if he was more embarrassed or angry.

"Well, she's a girl and a friend, and she's welcome to join us." His mom began clearing the table and Danny joined in.

In order to prove what he had said to his mom, he refused to invite Janey even though he would have liked to. Scoops Ice Cream was spilling its customers out onto the sidewalk. It was in the corner of an old brick building with a law office and a nail place. Bugs swarmed the halo of the streetlight above in a way that reminded Danny of the townspeople below.

They got their ice creams after a twenty-minute wait and

stood eating them on the sidewalk. They were arguing about the best flavor ever invented when a familiar voice came from behind Danny.

"Hello, Mrs. Owens."

Danny spun around and nearly dropped his cone.

Ms. Rait appeared to be alone, and she smiled at Danny's mom like they were old friends.

"I'm Martha Rait, Danny's English teacher." She extended her non-crutch hand. She wore a loose T-shirt and cutoff shorts, although her leg with a brace had some kind of sock that went up over her knee.

Danny's mom looked at the teacher's hand, confused and apparently angry, before she remembered her manners and shook it. "Yes, I've heard about you."

"Not all bad, I hope." Ms. Rait laughed lightly and looked from Danny to his mom.

"You're new here," Danny's mom said. "Strangers always get the benefit of the doubt."

"Doubt?" Ms. Rait tilted her head.

"Sometimes small towns have different ways of doing things

is all." Danny's mom licked around her ice cream. "I'm sure you'll figure how to fit in."

Ms. Rait chuckled. "I'm not sure what you even mean, but . . . oh, here's my ice cream."

She turned to the side and accepted a small vanilla cone from none other than Mr. Crenshaw.

Mr. Crenshaw passed off the cone with care, making sure Ms. Rait had a good hold before he turned to Danny and his mom. "Hi, Danny, is this your mom? Hi, Mrs. Owens. Bob Crenshaw. We spoke on the phone."

Danny's mom seemed as surprised and suspicious as he was. What was the counselor doing with the teacher who was giving him a hard time?

While Ms. Rait seemed like she had something to say, Mr. Crenshaw cut her off. "It's always nice to put a face with a name, isn't it? You two have a good night."

Crenshaw took Ms. Rait's arm and gently led her away down the sidewalk. They hadn't gone far before he said something to her that made them both laugh. Danny and his mom watched them until they turned the corner.

"Strange," his mom said.

Danny finished his ice cream in the car. The teacher and the counselor made him uneasy. He couldn't say why, until early the next morning when he and his mom walked into the principal's office to find the two of them together again.

Coach Kinen held out a chair for Danny's mom. She took it. Danny sat between her and Coach Kinen. Across from them were Ms. Rait and Mr. Crenshaw. Mr. Trufant was at the head of the table, and he cleared his throat.

"So," he said. "We have a situation, and I'd like to work it out without too much of a fuss, but—in the best interests of Danny and our other students—we do need to get things straight. Ms. Rait, Danny has struggled with English, and the teachers before now have understood and made accommodations. I don't want to simply pull some kind of power play when a nice discussion could set things straight. Am I being clear enough here?"

Ms. Rait sat with her hands folded in her lap. Her dark eyes seem to shine. "Danny can't read."

"Now, wait a minute . . ." Mr. Crenshaw looked at her in

disbelief. "Martha, we talked about this."

Ms. Rait held up a hand to silence him and she looked around the table. "Everyone's talked to me about this. 'Push him through English.' 'Don't make waves.' 'Danny's special. He could make it to the big time.' Well, I'm a reading teacher, and I want to teach him to read."

Coach Kinen pointed a finger at Mr. Crenshaw. "You said she was on board."

"She was." Mr. Crenshaw glanced at Ms. Rait. "She is."

"No," Ms. Rait said with a bitter smile. "I'm not. Not like that. What I will do is work with him."

They all sat in the stunned silence before Ms. Rait addressed Coach Kinen. "I'll work hard, and Danny will have to work hard, but if we work together, I think he can pass the first marking period so he can play in your precious championship game."

"And what if he doesn't pass?" Coach Kinen asked with a snarl. "You have no idea what's at stake for this young man. The county title is the game the varsity coaches will see. The big game could put him on a track that ends with him maybe even being a first-round draft pick. That's what he wants, and his momma, too."

She shrugged. "If he doesn't pass, he gets an F. After that, it's up to you all. I could care less if you want to make an exception that allows him to play football. Those aren't my rules. My rules are: a student has to meet minimum requirements for me to give a passing grade. Anything less and I wouldn't be doing my job, and I promise you that just won't happen."

"Have you thought about *having* a job?" Mr. Trufant's face

had gone from red to redder as she spoke. "You don't even have tenure, young lady."

Ms. Rait set her jaw and narrowed her eyes at the principal. "I was a unanimous selection by this school board, and unfortunately for me, I am also protected by the Americans with Disabilities Act. With all due respect, you don't want to fight that fight with me, sir."

Mr. Trufant's entire bald head had turned purple now, but he wasn't finished. He pushed his steel-rimmed glasses up on his nose and then patted a folder on the table in front of him before removing a sheet of paper with some official-looking writing on it. He took out a pen and signed it before pushing it toward Danny's mom along with his fancy pen.

When Mr. Trufant looked up, Danny could see the strain in his face. "I somehow anticipated you might prove to be a problem, Ms. Rait. Fortunately, I know how to work around problems. Mrs. Owens, this is a class transfer form. You just sign it alongside my signature and we can end this charade."

Danny's mom blinked and picked up the pen, which was nearly as thick as her index finger.

"Mrs. Owens, do not sign that paper. I will teach him to *read*." Ms. Rait looked like a woman possessed. She thumped her fist on the tabletop, and she spoke in a low, authoritative voice. "If you sign that, you're signing Danny's whole life away."

Danny's mom looked over at him and he silently begged her to sign.

"I . . ." Danny's mom looked around the room. "I—I need to think."

The first bell rang and everyone, including Ms. Rait, jumped up. "I have a class. If you'll excuse me."

Her crutch complained like a small metal mouse as she made her way to the door. Mr. Crenshaw sprang up and opened it for her before she disappeared. Coach Kinen reached across Danny and rested a hand on his mom's arm. "Go ahead, Sharon. You go think about it. You'll do the right thing. Ms. Rait has no idea what's at stake. She never met someone like your Daniel. She doesn't even know the future he can have in football."

Danny's mom stood and gathered the paper, gazing down at Danny. "You all set here, honey?"

"Mom, you—"

"Stop, Danny. I need to think. We can talk tonight." His

mom's hands shook and sadness seemed to smother her. "I need some space."

"Okay," Danny said, and they watched her go.

"You're gonna be fine." Coach Kinen patted him on the back. "See you at practice, Danny."

"I believe you two have a counseling session." Mr. Trufant was still stiff and angry as he left the room.

"Want to wait here till the final bell?" Mr. Crenshaw asked. "So no one sees you going into my office?"

"That would be great," Danny said.

When the second bell rang, he followed Mr. Crenshaw into his office and slumped down on the couch next to the bookshelf.

"More reading today?" Mr. Crenshaw pointed at the books, and Danny searched his face to see if he was making fun of him. It didn't look that way, and Danny relaxed a bit.

"My friend Janey said I should talk to you."

"Only when you're ready." Mr. Crenshaw went to the game shelf, took down a box, and sat at the table. "Yahtzee?"

"I have no idea what that is," Danny said.

"I can teach you." He removed a small red cup from the box and loaded it with five dice before rattling them around and dumping them out. "Look, three sixes. That's an awesome first roll."

Danny actually enjoyed the game. He quickly saw how calculating the odds could guide a smart player. With that and a little luck, he won by just three points on his final roll. "Yes!"

"Haha! Well done," said Mr. Crenshaw. "Played like an expert."

"Yeah, math is my thing." Danny grinned.

"Unlike reading."

Danny stiffened. "That's how this works? You get me off balance, then throw a zinger?"

Mr. Crenshaw sat back in his chair. "Why is that a zinger?"

"Whose side are you on here? Hers? Is she your girlfriend?"

"My personal life is off-limits." Mr. Crenshaw's eyes went briefly cold. "As far as a side, we're all on your side, Danny. If we didn't care, there'd be no problem."

"Really?" Danny huffed. "You try to fail someone and wreck his football career before it even gets started? That's not being on my side."

"Ms. Rait *wants* you to pass. We all do. But she wants you to do it on your own. Reading is something you'll need for the rest of your life."

"I can read." Danny glared. "I'm just not great at it. No one else has a problem with how I am. I think that if you're on my side, you work with me."

"Ms. Rait is saying she'll work with you." Mr. Crenshaw threw his hands in the air.

"Not like that." Danny thought that what Ms. Rait talked about would be impossible. Reading was a mystery he'd simply given up on. "Just get me through this. Not everyone's going to be a great reader. People are different, that's all."

"Imagine if you could read, though," Mr. Crenshaw said. "Even if you're a pro ballplayer, you'll have playbooks and scouting reports . . . and contracts."

Danny waved the idea away with the back of his hand. "I'll get people to do that for me."

Mr. Crenshaw stared at him for a moment, then rattled the dice. "How about another game?"

"Sure." Danny liked that Mr. Crenshaw wasn't going to nag him. He wasn't a bad guy, and Danny thought maybe first period with him wasn't going to be such a terrible thing. He didn't need study hall, really, and the tone he'd set by pummeling Markle had benefits as well. He could tell by the way his teammates looked at him in the halls and in the locker room that they were wary of him. They respected him, maybe even feared him, which, in the game of football, wasn't bad.

All in all, things would work out fine.

In his mind, he saw his mom doing the right thing, just like Coach Kinen talked about. She'd go home and settle down and sign the release. With a new English teacher, he'd be right back where he should be.

Danny kept his head high as he walked into English class and sat down behind Janey. He was somewhat sad that when he got the new teacher he wouldn't be with her for English anymore, and not just because she helped him. But Danny knew the road to the NFL was a rough one, and he knew he'd have to make even bigger sacrifices in the future.

Ms. Rait didn't pay him any special attention, but she did hand out a test first thing after the bell. Danny took his and passed the rest back. He flipped through the two-page test, circling random answers and calculating the odds. He wondered how much higher, or lower, he'd get than the probable 25 percent.

Finished before anyone else, he looked around. When he caught Ms. Rait's eye, he smiled pleasantly. Not smug, just pleasant. He didn't want to rub it in, but it was hard not to recall the color of Mr. Trufant's face when he asked her if she'd like to keep her job.

The tests were handed in and they spent the rest of class talking about the kid in the book, Bud, who didn't like to be called Buddy. It was the opposite for Danny. When people called him Dan, he used to look around to see if they were talking to his dad.

That made him think of the way Coach Kinen said "Daniel" in their meeting with the principal. Danny felt the icy grip of horror on his heart and immediately turned his mind back to reading . . . it was definitely overrated. Everything was in video on a screen now.

When the bell rang, he ignored the teacher and bolted from the room.

"Hey, Danny, wait up!" Janey called out in the hallway.

"Last time I'll have to see her," he said to Janey when she caught up.

"What do you mean?" she asked.

He told her the story about the meeting, but when he looked to see her reaction, she kept her head angled down and continued walking.

"Isn't it great?" He stopped and tugged at her arm.

"I like having you in English." She smiled weakly. "And she said she'd teach you. Isn't that an opportunity?"

He let go of her arm. His mouth dropped. "An opportunity to *fail*. What's wrong with you?"

"I'm sorry, Danny. I think you should be able to read. I've told you that before."

"Yeah, but in a nice way, like you were on my side. Not

this. This is risking my whole football career." He couldn't believe what she was saying. More than anyone, Janey knew how important the big game was. The chance to catch Coach Oglethorpe's eye. She knew it was the path his father had taken, and she knew Danny was determined to follow that same path. It was his mission in life.

"Calm down. I'm just saying . . ."

"Well, don't." He forced a laugh, like it was simply poor humor on her part. "Don't talk crazy. I need you."

"Need me?"

He looked into her eyes. "You're my best friend."

"I know." The bell rang and she looked up. "I can't help what I feel though. I gotta go."

Danny watched her leave without trying to stop her.

"Girls," he said, sounding like he didn't care what she thought, even though he did.

He and Janey still sat together with Cupcake at lunch, but they didn't talk about reading anymore.

The rest of the day passed, and Danny had a strong practice after school, earning Coach Kinen's praise. But when Cupcake's brother pulled the pickup truck into his driveway, Danny had a sinking feeling in his chest.

He threw open the back door and stopped just inside. His mother sat at the table with an unlit cigarette in her mouth, fists clenched. She was staring at the pen and paper in front of her. She looked up at him with fire in her eyes, removed the cigarette, and said, "Good, you're home."

Then she picked up the pen and signed the classroom transfer.

"Thank you, Mom." Danny hugged his mom. "Thank you!"

"Now you gotta make it, Danny." She rubbed the back of his head. "I know you can. You've got everything your father had and more. You were born for this. Don't you let me down."

"I won't, Mom. I won't."

They had dinner. She'd roasted a chicken and mashed some potatoes. Danny had a tall glass of milk and then she brought a peach pie from the kitchen. He was cutting into his second piece when his mom raised her head after a sip of coffee.

"Is that someone in the driveway?"

Danny listened.

His mom got up and went to the window, pushing aside the curtain just as the front doorbell rang. It was a sound they rarely heard because everyone they knew came in through the kitchen.

Danny's mom wrinkled her nose and went to open the door. "Who could that be?"

Danny stuffed a big bite of pie into his mouth. His mom swung open the front door and froze.

"Oh!" There was a pause as his mom recovered her senses. "Ms. Rait, can I help you?"

Danny dropped his fork.

"Would you mind if I came in and sat down?" Ms. Rait's voice was clear and strong.

Danny quickly flipped the classroom transfer form face-down on the table. He realized his mouth was full, and as Ms. Rait came into sight, he chewed and tried to swallow, but the pie got stuck. He gulped some milk to wash it down and began to choke.

"Danny?" His mom frowned.

Danny raised his hand to hold her off, ashamed, and tried to keep the whole mess from flying out his nose.

"Oh dear," said Ms. Rait. She quickly closed the gap, braced herself on the crutch, and gave Danny's back a careful thump with her free hand.

A glob of pie popped out of his mouth and plunked down on the tabletop. He immediately covered the mess with his napkin and wiped it up, his face warm with embarrassment.

"Happens to the best of us." Ms. Rait pulled a chair out from the table with her free hand and sat down with a smile as pleasant as if she were an invited guest. "Now, we need to talk, and I'm glad it's the three of us. I want you both to know that I am completely on your side. You never should have gotten to this point, Danny, but here you are, and it's past time to fix the problem. Good news is: we can do it. Bad news is: it won't be easy. You have to do the work. And you have to be able to read—no more copying from someone else."

She looked back and forth between Danny and his mom. "So, should we start tomorrow?"

Danny and his mom were silent for a few moments. Then Danny's mom cleared her throat. "Thank you for your concern, and thank you for helping Danny just now, but we are going in a different direction."

"Different?" Ms. Rait blinked at them.

"Football is in his blood. His father was a Super Bowl champion." Danny's mom pointed to the framed photo on the mantel above the fireplace.

Ms. Rait squinted.

"Let me show you something."

Danny's mom walked into the living room and returned with the framed picture of his father with the Super Bowl trophy.

"They call this the Lombardi Trophy. My Daniel scored two touchdowns." She offered it to the teacher with two hands as if it were a religious relic passed down over thousands of years.

"Oh," said Ms. Rait. "How nice. The Steelers."

Danny's mom puffed up. "Danny's father was a third-round draft pick."

"I'm sorry, I don't know what that means." Danny could tell by the teacher's face that she was serious.

Danny's mom took back the picture, almost as if Ms. Rait didn't deserve to hold it. Walking fast, she replaced it on the mantel, next to a Steelers helmet. When she came back she said, "You have no idea what it means to be a football player."

"No, I don't," Ms. Rait said. "But then, even if you play, you still need something to do when it ends, and there aren't many things you can do if you can't read."

Danny's mom braced her hands on the tabletop and leaned toward the teacher like a judge rendering a decision. "Danny's father always said his son would be even better than he was. He was aiming for Danny to be a first-round pick."

Ms. Rait absorbed that before she said, "Danny could get hurt in high school and never even get a college scholarship."

His mom's hands flew into the air. "He could get hit by a car and none of it matters, right? We're not talking about what *could* happen, we're talking about what *should* happen. My son is on track for something very special, and as well intentioned as you may be, you're throwing up a roadblock in front of his destiny. Everyone seems to see that but you."

Ms. Rait turned to Danny. "You're pretty good at math. There are one million high school football players. Someone told me only three hundred of them will get drafted into the NFL."

Danny opened his mouth to speak, but his mom beat him to it. "Danny's not just another player. Danny Owens is special. Ask Coach Kinen. Ask anyone. He's Dan Owens's son."

"We're talking about maybe missing one game," the teacher said. "I don't think he'll miss even that, but if he did, and he is as good as you say he is, one game shouldn't matter."

"It's the big game," Danny explained. "The *championship*. Coach Oglethorpe and his staff from the high school will see it, and sometimes they take a young player for their varsity team next season. They don't care about the other games. They only want a young kid if he proves he can perform under championship pressure."

"Let me ask you a question." Danny's mom scowled at Ms. Rait. "You care so much about my son, why don't you just help him learn to read and agree to pass him, too? What's so hard about that?"

Ms. Rait took a long time before she spoke. "That's how we got to this point, Mrs. Owens. Everyone wants to help Danny. He's nice and polite and good looking. He's a star athlete whose dad won the Super Bowl. So when Danny struggled, they 'helped' him. They passed him on. Let him cheat. And now he's twelve and he can't read.

"This isn't your fault. It's the school's fault. This kind of thing happens when people are too afraid or too lazy to do their jobs. I am neither afraid nor lazy, and Danny needs to know that he has to do this. No faking. No cheating. No passing grades unless he *really* passes."

Danny's mom pointed at the paper on the table in front of Danny. Danny glanced at the peach pie skid mark.

"I already signed it," his mom said.

"Yes, I know," said Ms. Rait. "I can see the imprint of two

signatures. The idea of playing in the NFL is very exciting. But it ends, doesn't it? Then what?"

Danny's mom didn't say anything, and Danny thought Ms. Rait would leave. But the teacher pointed to the paper and said, "You signed it. The big question is, what will you do with it?"

Danny stared at the second piece of pie, the one he'd never finish. He listened through a fog of disbelief as his mom promised he'd be at Ms. Rait's house tomorrow after practice to begin work. He raised a stiff hand and mumbled goodbye as the teacher headed toward the front door. He heard his mom thanking her before closing it.

Danny scowled at his mom. "Why?"

"Because she's right." His mom picked up the transfer paper and tore it into shreds before sprinkling it into the trash bin. "This will only make you better, Danny, stronger. You'll have options. There's no reason you shouldn't have options. The more I think about it, the more I realize that we're lucky she came along."

Danny pushed back his chair and marched into his room,

slamming the door. He had no idea what to do. He had no interest in the Xbox or his airplane model. He called Janey and told her what had happened.

"Can you believe it?" he said with outrage. "My own mom?"

Janey was silent.

"Janey? You there?"

"Yes," she replied quickly.

"I said, can you believe it?"

"I know. I heard the first time." Janey sighed. "I guess, yes, I can believe it."

"Why?"

She huffed. "I've been telling you, Danny. You just never listened, but think about how many times I tried to get you to do the homework *with* me instead of just copying mine."

He couldn't argue with that, but he'd come to think of it as a running joke, not something she was serious about. "I can't even believe you're selling me out."

"I'm not selling you out." Her anger crackled over the phone. "Stop feeling sorry for yourself and just get this done. Think of it like training. Dig in. Get tough."

"This isn't training. It's school stuff, and it's easy for you to say because you get it. Well, I don't!"

He hung up before Janey could respond and got onto his Xbox instead. Cupcake was more than willing to listen, and he was firmly on Danny's side.

"And listen to this," Cupcake said, "I know you don't do Facebook, but Jace posted on our team page that we all gotta stick together and that's the only way to win a championship."

"Nice, but what's that got to do with me and Rait?"

"Bro, we stick together. When everyone hears about this—which is total barley—I can see us doing, like, some protests or something."

"Well, I can't do that," Danny said. "My mom would kill me."

"That's the beauty of it. *You* don't do anything," Cupcake said, excited. "You just leave it to the team."

The next day, Danny was pleasantly surprised when Mr. Crenshaw didn't ask him about the Rait thing. Danny didn't bring it up because he was testing the counselor to see if he could mind his own business. They played Yahtzee all first period, and Mr. Crenshaw said he'd see Danny tomorrow.

In English class, Ms. Rait carried on like *Bud, Not Buddy* was the Bible or something. Danny stifled his yawns, but he had nothing to say, and Ms. Rait didn't give him so much as a sideways look. Janey was into the story and had her hand up for every question the teacher asked. At one point, it was almost like the two of them were having a private discussion.

Danny was almost out the door after class when Ms. Rait called his name. He cringed and gave Janey a frustrated look before turning back.

"I know you have to get to your next class, but this is for you." Ms. Rait reached into her desk drawer and took out something like a square stopwatch on a lanyard. Then she took out some earbuds and plugged them into it. "It's a Playaway."

"What?"

"A Playaway. It's an audio book reader. It's got *Bud, Not*

103

Buddy on it." She held it out to him and showed him how to turn it on and use the simple buttons. "Reading isn't just about reading. It's about stories of people and the obstacles they overcome."

Danny didn't know what to say.

"Take it, Danny. Try it. It'll fit in your pocket."

He stuffed it in. "Okay. Thank you."

"See you after practice."

"Yes, ma'am." He left feeling something between annoyed and thankful. When he got lunch from his locker he stuffed the Playaway into his backpack and wondered if he'd even use it.

At the end of the day there was a study period before sports practices began. Kids who had detention went to a silent classroom and the rest either sought extra help from teachers, went to the library, or sat in the cafeteria for what they called "sports study hall." Danny typically sat with Cupcake and Janey, but today his two friends had to go to an extra lab for the science class they shared, so he opted for the library. He had one math sheet to do. It was all numbers, so he found a study carrel in the corner and knocked it off, feeling good.

He looked around to see that no one was looking before taking the Playaway from his backpack and plugging the buds into his ears. After another check for people who might see him, he began the story.

It got under his skin right away. This boy, this sad, lonely orphan with no parents and no home, was someone Danny could root for. It made his own problems seem smaller, and when the bell rang announcing the end of the study session, he was reluctant to turn the Playaway off.

He certainly wasn't going to let any of his teammates see him with it, though, so back into the pack it went before he left the library.

Inside the locker room, there was an unusual hush, as if everyone was waiting for something. It only took Danny half a minute to look around and realize they'd been waiting for him.

Jace walked to the open area in the middle of the locker room.

"Danny." The team captain spoke in a somber voice. "Come here."

Danny had his school clothes off and wore just his padded girdle. His bare feet felt clammy as he walked across the grungy tile floor. He straightened his back and clenched his fists, having no idea what was about to happen. He thought Jace liked him, but it sure didn't seem that was the case now.

"Now we all know that seventh graders . . ." Jace scowled around at the entire team. "Are dirt."

The eighth-grade players howled and banged their hands against the metal lockers in agreement. Danny had no idea where this was going, but he knew he'd fight Jace if he had to.

Jace held his hands up and the locker room went silent. "Tomorrow, the season begins. Today, we clean up the dirt."

Wild cheers from the eighth graders, until Jace held up his hands again. "The eighth graders all know it's tradition that the seventh graders get cleaned through the gauntlet. Like the gauntlet on the field, it's punishing. The seventh graders will walk through the gauntlet and the eighth graders will smack their backsides. And, once the dirt is cleaned up, we're one team. But to do that we can't have any grudges. No bad feelings remain. The seventh graders need to accept their punishment like men."

"Yeah!" Every eighth grader screamed his assent.

"This season, we also have a special situation, a bitter grudge between a seventh and an eighth grader." Jace turned a cold eye on Danny. "And it requires a special, individual punishment to clear the air."

Danny saw some pushing and shoving from the corner of his eye and he looked over to see Markle emerge from the crowd between some lockers. He had his football pants on and a sleeveless half T-shirt that showed off his ab and arm muscles. His long hair was tied back, exposing his purple-welted face.

Even the swelling around Markle's eyes and nose couldn't hide the broad smile as he stepped up to Danny, steadily smacking a fist into his open hand.

"Danny, hold out your hands." Jace held out his own hands as an example, palms up.

"Why?"

"Hold out your hands!" Jace's face burned red.

Danny felt the sweat steaming from his armpits. He trembled, not with fear, but rage. He somehow knew Markle was going to slap or punch his open hands. He wanted to scream how stupid that would be. What if it truly hurt his hands? He had to play tomorrow.

"Let's go!" Jace barked.

Danny nodded. "Okay."

Markle gave Danny a wicked smile.

Danny held out his hands, but not because he was going along. He didn't give a rat's behind what people thought.

When Markle went to slap his hands, Danny was going to punch him in the face, again.

Danny and Markle stared each other down. With his eyes, Danny tried to warn Markle, but the older boy kept grinning.

"Okay," Markle announced, "here's your punishment, seventh grader: you gotta hug it out with me."

A smattering of uncomfortable laughter bounced off the lockers like a handful of pennies.

Danny's muscles tightened. He was ready, but now uncertain. "What?"

Markle seemed to be having fun. "Yeah, that's right. Hug it out. Put it behind us. Move on. We can be cool, right?"

"Us?"

"Yup. C'mon. C'mere." Markle stepped forward and hugged Danny, thumping his back with a meaty hand.

Danny went stiff, but when he realized Markle was serious and not pulling some stunt, he let his arms embrace his teammate and he patted his back like a small dog's.

Jace laughed out loud. "That's it. Some serious punishment to have to hug it out with Markle!"

The rest of the team laughed too.

"All right!" Jace shouted. "Two lines for the gauntlet! Owens, you're first, and then we hit the field and get ready to stomp Froston!"

They whooped and hollered and made two lines. The eighth graders began to clap their hands in sync against their thighs.

"You go through slow, or you go through again!" Jace bellowed through the cheering noise.

Danny braced himself and took a step into the gauntlet. He was halfway through when he began laughing. They weren't smacking his butt using their hands as heavy paddles. They were giving the light smacks you gave someone when they scored a touchdown.

Cupcake came out of the end right after Danny. He leaned close to Danny's ear. "That didn't even hurt."

"I don't think it's supposed to," Danny said.

"They said punishment." Cupcake scratched his flattop. More seventh graders were coming out, all wearing silly grins.

"Yeah," Danny said. "I got a hug and you got a pat on your bum."

"Well, it beats bloody knuckles and sitting on a pillow." Cupcake slapped another teammate high five.

When it was finished, the whole team bounced up and down, woofing like dogs, until Jace shouted, "Break it down!" And they roared like one giant beast.

When they were all dressed in their gear, they marched

down to the field in two columns and circled around their coaches.

"Take a knee!" Coach Kinen barked. "So, you seventh graders went through the team gauntlet. Now we're one. Next year, you'll do the same thing to the new class, so don't tell anyone. It's a tradition, and we do it that way to make it scary. The unknown is always scary. Then, you find out that the guys doing the gauntlet are your teammates, and they don't hurt you, they help you. They congratulate you for making it to the regular season, where the enemy is anyone we play. Right?"

"Right, Coach!" they yelled as one.

"That's right." Coach smiled at them. "And the game tomorrow is gonna be like a gauntlet for you seventh graders. You don't know what to expect. You're nervous, but this team is gonna be with you. You'll be fine. You'll be together, supporting each other, and we *will* win!"

They cheered and Coach Kinen blew his whistle and practice began. It was an easy day, with no hitting or wind sprints. They ran through plays, making sure everyone knew his job, and when it ended, Danny wasn't tired in the least. He was flying high, eager to begin his junior high football career.

He forgot all about Ms. Rait and her reading lesson. He and Cupcake were in Herman's truck, stopped at the light in town, when Danny was torn from their joking conversation as he remembered his appointment with the teacher.

"Hey, sorry, Herman. Can you pull over and let me out?"

Herman stroked his thick beard and gave Danny a funny look. "Right here?"

"Yeah, I gotta do some extra schoolwork at my teacher's house."

"That's barley," said Cupcake.

The light turned green. Herman made his turn but pulled over. "Want me to take you to wherever you're going?"

"Nah. I can walk." Danny was already out the door, and he shouted his thanks before slamming it shut.

Cupcake rolled down his window. "This with Rait?"

Danny paused. "Yeah, but no big deal."

Danny had filled him in at lunch about the teacher's conditions.

Cupcake hung his arm out the window. "Well, how you gonna get home? Walk five miles?"

"Ms. Rait drops me off. I'm fine. We'll play *Siege* later, after dinner."

"Well, okay," Cupcake said. "Don't forget, I talked to Jace and the guys say they'll run her out of town if she messes with you."

"Yeah. I'm okay," Danny said, wondering how they'd even do something like that.

Cupcake saluted, then said something to his brother, and they pulled away.

Danny shouldered his pack and crossed the intersection. He trudged through town until the houses thinned out. He passed several fields and some woods before he came to an old farmhouse with number 1197 on the mailbox.

It was a trim little two-story white house with a green roof and shutters. The barns had been torn down, but an old red chicken coop stood off to the side out back. Several live oak trees surrounded the house providing shade. Gravel crunched beneath Danny's feet.

Ms. Rait's car was parked beside the house, and he now saw she'd had a ramp built to give her access to the front porch without having to climb the stairs that Danny took. There was a sidelight window next to the door, and he peered through it to see what he could see as he reached for the bell.

He looked down a hallway and into the kitchen on the back side of the house. Ms. Rait was sitting at the table with a tall glass of iced tea. She wasn't alone.

He pulled his finger back from the bell, because this was definitely not part of the deal.

Ms. Rait saw him and waved her hand like a bat's wing, crazy and fast.

Janey turned and saw him too, and she was up out of her seat before he could run. He knew it was her from her ponytail, and he had to wonder how deeply she was involved in this whole reading thing. Had she betrayed him from the start? It bruised his heart to even think that.

The door flew open.

"Hi, Danny." Janey's voice didn't have even a hint of guilt.

"I . . . what are you doing here?"

"I saw Ms. Rait after volleyball practice. She was carrying some books and I helped her get them into her car and she asked me over for tea." Janey smiled like this was an ordinary thing to happen. "Come in."

It felt like some kind of a setup, but it was Janey, so he followed her into a bright kitchen with tree-filtered light falling in through the lace curtains on the windows. The walls and cabinets were white, as was the floor; the only color came from some blue tiles here and there and the blue jars on the countertops.

There was a third drinking glass, empty, on the table. Ms. Rait raised a clear pitcher with ice and lemon slices floating in the tea.

"Can I pour you a glass, Danny?" she asked.

"Yes, ma'am. Thank you." Danny sat down, accepted the cool glass, and took a sip.

"We like it lemony and sweet." Ms. Rait smiled at Janey. "I hope that's okay."

"Yes, ma'am, it's real good."

"Janey tells me the two of you are thick as thieves." Ms. Rait raised her glass.

"Ma'am?" The word "thieves" alarmed him.

She laughed. "It's an old-fashioned way of saying best friends. The kind that would do anything for each other. Is that right?"

Danny glanced at Janey. The freckles on her round cheeks stood out from her blush and she cast her hazel eyes at the floor as she slipped into her seat.

"Pretty much," Danny said.

"So, I thought it would be okay if she stays while we do some testing. Would you be more comfortable with her here?"

"I guess so, yes," Danny said. "Why do I have to take a test?

You already know I can't read good."

Ms. Rait reached down into a shoulder bag she had beside her chair. She removed a folder full of papers and set it on the round wooden table. "I need to drill down on exactly what's going on with your reading. Then I'll know how to fix it. I think I know, just from when you said 'toe' instead of 'to.' I think you have gaps in your phonetic awareness."

"That doesn't sound good." Danny's throat tightened.

"It's not that bad, really. If you have to have a reading problem, it's the best one to have." She opened the folder and slid a stapled bunch of papers his way. "It means you recognize letters and their sounds but just have a tough time stringing the sounds together in the right way. With some hard work, we can fix it in a short time, but let's not get ahead of ourselves. Let me make sure I'm right."

Danny took a pen from his backpack, flipped the first page over, and began. There were letters and pictures that he had to match them to. It was easy until he came to a page with whole words; then he began to melt down.

After that, Ms. Rait held up cards and asked him to read the words. He got a few simple ones but butchered the rest. Same thing with his writing. She asked him to spell some simple words she spoke aloud, and it was ugly.

Janey saw his face and she patted his hand. "You're fine. It's all good, Danny. Really good."

He could tell by her eyes that she meant it, and he kept going. After the written part, Ms. Rait held up more cards for him with just letters, then letter combinations, and finally whole words that made him struggle again.

"It's just what I thought, Danny." Ms. Rait tucked the papers and cards back into the folder, then swapped it for a different folder. She took out a single sheet along with some blank index cards. "These are 'sight words,' words you can't always sound out, but important words you need to memorize."

The page full of words reminded Danny of when he first saw the gauntlet machine on the field.

"Let's go through them. Read me the words you know and we'll circle the ones you don't so you can work on them."

Danny knew many of the words on the first sheet, words like "and," "the," and "this." He struggled mightily with the second sheet though, which had bigger words like "agree," "flour," and "thrill."

"You make flash cards for the circled ones," said Ms. Rait. "We can take a few each day for you to memorize. You won't learn them all at once, but you can learn them. I know you can."

"Well, I know this one is 'tap.'" Danny pointed to the word. "So this should be 'tack.'" This time he pointed to "take."

Ms. Rait nodded. "Okay, but that's 'take.' The 'a' sounds like its name, 'a,' because of the 'e' at the end. That's a silent 'e.' When silent 'e' comes at the end of the word, the vowel makes a long sound and says its name. I know it can be confusing, but vowels can make different sounds. So that the same 'a' can make more than just the 'a' sound when it's in other words. It can also sound like 'uh,' as in 'about.' Most of the time though 'a' makes the sound you hear in 'tap' or 'ax' or 'tack.' So, when you see an 'a' I want you to think 'tap,' *unless* you see that silent

116

'e' at the end. Then I want you to say the word aloud, then ask yourself two questions: Does that sound right? Does that make sense in the sentence?"

Danny nodded slowly. "Okay. I think I get that."

"And I can help you with the flash cards." Janey rattled the ice in her glass.

"Let me show you some," Ms. Rait said. "I think it's easier when you can see it."

Danny did see it, and he began to say words right he hadn't known before. He laughed out loud, and then he heard a noise from the corner of the kitchen. Ms. Rait had a pet door cut into the lower part of the back door, and an enormously fat white cat wiggled its way inside.

"Oh, Mrs. McGillicuddy, where have you been?" Ms. Rait was up out of her chair now and she expertly thumped across the kitchen to the fridge, where she took out a carton of milk and poured some into a pan by the garbage can.

The cat pattered across the floor and began drinking. Ms. Rait sat back down.

"That's a big cat," Janey said.

"That's a pregnant cat," said Ms. Rait, and then she sighed. "But she's fat too."

They went over a few more sight words and the sounds Ms. Rait wanted Danny to use for other vowels before Mrs. McGillicuddy began to circle Danny's leg, rubbing her head against his shinbone.

Ms. Rait peered under the table. "She's shameless. Loves men and makes no bones about it."

Danny and Janey laughed.

"Can I pick her up?" Danny asked.

"Only if you want to make her day," said Ms. Rait. "I think we've done enough work."

Danny scooped the large cat up into his lap, and she collapsed there in a fluffy heap. Danny laughed and scratched her ears. She began to purr faster and pressed her head into his fingers for more.

"Told you," Ms. Rait said.

"I like this cat." Danny stroked her long white fur.

"Do you have a cat?" Ms. Rait asked.

"No, my mom's a dog person. We had a dog, but it got hit by a car. My mom cried for a week and said 'never again.'"

"Well, Mrs. McGillicuddy has decided *you* are a cat person." Ms. Rait folded her hands on the table. "Now, what can you tell me about this football team of yours? I already know our girls' volleyball team is the best in the county."

Janey blushed. "Well, one of the best for sure."

"Same with football." Danny dove right in and told Ms. Rait all about Jericho High and how Crooked Creek Junior High was the main source of talent for Jericho. He talked until Mrs. McGillicuddy hopped down off his lap and headed for the pet door. She got stuck halfway through and began to yowl.

"Can you give her a push, Danny?" Ms. Rait asked.

Danny went over to the door and with two hands gently stuffed the cat through the swinging door. When he straightened up, he saw Mrs. McGillicuddy dash across the grass and up into the chicken coop.

"That chicken coop reminds me of the Amoses' shed." Danny pointed out the window in the upper half of the door.

"Amoses?" Janey said.

"From *Bud, Not Buddy*. The shed with the fish heads and the wasps."

"But . . ." Janey looked confused.

Danny laughed and dug the Playaway out of his backpack. He told her about how Ms. Rait had given it to him.

"It sounds like you like it," the teacher said.

"I did," said Danny. "I do."

"See?" Ms. Rait sounded excited, the way she did in class. "Those details you just told us about? Inside the shed? That's called reading comprehension."

Danny frowned. "But I didn't read it."

"That's right. You *heard* it, but it doesn't matter how you get the information, through your eyes or your ears; you still understood it and remembered it and connected it with real life. That's just excellent."

Danny wasn't sure if he should feel incredibly proud about all that, but he did have to fight to keep a smile from curling his lips.

"Anyway, I think that old coop is where Mrs. McGillicuddy has made a den for her future kittens. And if either of you wants one, you're welcome."

"How many will she have?" Janey asked.

"At her age? Four or five at least."

They packed up their things and talked about whether their parents would let them have a kitten and what they'd name their new pets if they were allowed. Ms. Rait dropped them off, Janey first. When she pulled into Danny's driveway, he got out, but before closing the door he said, "Ms. Rait, why are you doing all this?"

She looked at him, surprised. "You really don't know?"

Danny shook his head.

"I'm a teacher, Danny. It's what teachers do." Ms. Rait raised her hands off the wheel and shrugged. "Listen, I want to be honest with you. Today was easy. Having Janey there, and testing you, giving you some sight words and introducing you to vowel sounds, was like a summer picnic. I'm gonna push you, Danny. You might not like me tomorrow the way you like me right now."

"That's okay, Ms. Rait. I'm a football player. I'm used to coaches being tough on me. I can take it."

She nodded. "I'll remind you of that."

"Oh, and about tomorrow . . ." Danny met her eyes.

"Yes?" She raised her eyebrows.

"So, I've got a game."

"Yes, I know. We'll have to work in the evening. I can do that, though."

Danny hesitated. "Yeah, but it's game day. We should probably just skip game days. I'm gonna be gassed. It takes a lot out of you. Especially if I'm carrying the ball a lot, which is what happens pretty much all the time."

Ms. Rait's mouth flattened. "I'm sorry. Either you're not listening, or you're not taking me seriously. I know I asked you about your team, but I don't care about football, Danny. I care about education and reading, not touchdowns and . . . sideline sweepers, or whatever it is you do. In eight weeks, you're going to take my first-term final. By yourself. You fail and you'll be ineligible for football. If we work every day between now and then, you might not fail. If you're not interested in that kind of commitment, please let me know now so I don't waste my time."

Danny blinked. It didn't seem possible that she'd transformed from some sweet lady into a total witch in just seconds, but apparently she had.

He gritted his teeth. "Okay then. Tomorrow after the game it is."

"Seven thirty works perfectly," she said, pleasant again.

"Yes, ma'am," he said, getting out and closing the car door.

He went inside and all his mom wanted to talk about was Ms. Rait. Danny didn't know what to say, so he basically said nothing, which irritated his mom and kept him from showing her the sight words sheet or telling her about the flash cards.

"She's got a nice cat," he finally said. "It's gonna have kittens and she said I could have one."

"No," his mom said.

"Why not?"

"I'll think about it."

Danny took that as a yes, and once he was safely inside his bedroom with the door locked, he sat down at his desk to try and do some work for Ms. Rait. He worked hard on "about," "take," "thrill," and "agree" and other words they'd gone over on the list, writing them out. He was feeling so proud of himself that he dug the classroom copy of *Bud, Not Buddy* from the pile of untouched schoolbooks on his desk and opened it up.

Immediately he began to drown in the words and letters on the page. He tossed the book, end over end, back onto the desk so it landed open-faced with its pages splayed out. He snatched up the word sheet and began pacing the room with it. He tried to figure the word "these" and came up with a dozen versions—he assumed all were wrong.

"Never." He grabbed his hair with both hands and breathed heavy through his nose.

Then he knew what to do.

He turned on the Xbox and joined Cupcake's party.

"Hey, bro! Where you been?" Cupcake said. "We got hostages to save. You ready?"

"Does a cow make milk?"

"Wahoo! Now we're talking! One hundred percent pure beef. Made in America, baby. Let's dance!"

They launched into a series of *Siege* matches until Danny's thumbs were tired. They were 3–3 when everyone decided they had to end the night with a winning record even though it was late. They got into a serious battle with another team that went into extra rounds. It went on so long that the game finally declared sudden death. It was about to begin when Danny's mom rapped her knuckles on the door.

"Danny? You've got a game tomorrow."

"I know." He muted his microphone, then raised his voice

so it'd make it through the door. "I'm getting off."

"You know your dad always said—"

"I don't want to hear what Dad always said!" Danny yelled with an intensity that surprised him maybe even more than his mother. He took a deep breath. "Look, Mom, can we talk about it tomorrow? I'm getting off and going to bed. All right?"

After a few seconds of stillness, Danny's mother said, "That's good, sweetheart. Get your rest."

Danny kept his mike muted. He laughed a crazy laugh, and when the round began, he systematically killed his own team, then pulled out a grenade and dropped it at his feet.

Boom!

The controller rattled in his hand and the TV shook from the sound of the impact.

His headset lit up with chatter.

"Danny!"

"What the heck was that?"

"You idiot!"

"He killed us."

"Danny, why?"

Danny held himself to keep from laughing his head right off. He powered down the Xbox to silence them.

"*Danny, why?*" he repeated in a high-pitched voice, mocking them.

As he shook with laughter, he realized that he had no idea why. And his laughter quickly disappeared.

The next morning Danny wore a dress shirt and a tie along with khaki pants.

Mr. Crenshaw raised his eyebrows. "Church this morning?"

Danny fidgeted with his tie and slumped down on the couch. "Coach Kinen says game days we have to dress for business."

"Ahh." Mr. C angled his head toward the game box resting on the coffee table in front of the couch. "Yahtzee?"

"You gotta get Xbox, Mr. C." Danny wrinkled his nose at Yahtzee, then chuckled at the thought of last night. He'd seen Cupcake in the hall and his friend had given him a dirty look and called him "barley boy" before turning his back. Danny knew he'd be over it by lunch.

"What's so funny?" Mr. C asked.

Danny told him how the game had ended last night. Instead

of laughing, Mr. C frowned. "How did that make you feel?"

Danny stiffened. "What do you mean?"

"To kill your friends and then yourself. I know it's only a video game, but you were happy, right? I mean, you're laughing now. You played a joke on your friends, I get that."

"I was happy, yeah. I guess. It was funny for a little while."

"So you felt something else, too," Mr. C said. "Maybe angry?"

Danny chewed on his bottom lip. "I guess . . . I was mad."

Mr. C nodded. "Yes."

Danny looked into the counselor's eyes.

"What made you mad?" Mr. Crenshaw spoke softly.

The room felt painfully quiet. Danny looked at his hands and shook his head.

"Where did that anger come from?" Mr. C asked softly again.

"I shot Cupcake first, so he couldn't see it coming. But the others . . . they just stood around and let me pop them. Why would you be so stupid?"

Mr. C picked up a pen and gently tapped his desk. "So you were angry at them for dying?"

Danny suddenly saw red. He swept the Yahtzee box off the table so hard it burst open and the dice scattered. He leaped up and kicked the table. "This is stupid! I don't have to be here! I don't have to read! Why don't you and your stupid girlfriend leave me alone?"

Danny raced out the door and let it stay open behind him. He stomped through the hallways and realized Mr. C was silently trailing him.

Danny stopped and shouted, "Stop following me. What are you doing?"

Mr. C shrugged, but he didn't seem upset. "You're my responsibility for first period. I'd prefer we stay in my office, but you're upset."

"No, I'm *not*!" Danny said.

"Okay."

Danny growled and marched to his locker. He opened it and took the Playaway from his backpack.

"Oh, that's a good idea," said the counselor. "Can you do that in my office?"

"No. I'm going outside to sit under a tree."

"That works."

Danny rolled his eyes. He marched right out the front entrance of the school, down the steps, and threw himself down in the grass under a big old tree. He put his back to its trunk and put the buds in his ears. He marveled at what he was getting away with. Mr. C might as well have been Cupcake for all the rules he was following—none.

Mr. C took out his phone and sat on the stone railing at the bottom of the steps. He seemed to pay Danny no mind, and after a while the story Danny was listening to got so good he forgot Mr. C was even there.

It was some time before he heard a shout that he ignored. He heard it two more times before he realized it was his name.

"Owens!"

Danny looked up and saw Mr. Trufant, red faced and trembling with rage. Danny yanked his earbuds out.

"What in the world are you doing out here?" the principal roared.

"Listening, sir."

"Well, listen to me . . . You just listened your way out of playing in a football game today."

29

"What?" Danny looked around in a panic.

Mr. Crenshaw was gone from his spot on the steps, but taking a wider look, Danny spied the counselor. He was strolling toward them from the teachers' parking lot like everything was just fine.

Mr. Trufant followed the direction of Danny's eyes and his mouth fell open in disbelief. He clumped down the steps. "Bob, what in the world are you doing out here?"

Mr. Crenshaw had a bright red apple in his hand. He tossed it in the air, caught it, and took a crunchy bite. "I was getting an apple from my car."

The principal puffed up, still scowling. "I see that. I mean what are you doing out here with *Danny*? I look out my office window and I see a student, missing from the building, unsupervised . . ."

Mr. Crenshaw didn't hurry nor did he speak until he stood directly in front of his boss. "Nature therapy."

"Nature what?"

"Therapy, nature therapy. Some people call it a derivative of transcendentalism, but it's very current." Mr. C turned to Danny. "Feeling better?"

"Uh, yes, sir."

"How about that?" Mr. Crenshaw snapped his fingers in the air as he breathed in deep. "Fresh air. The shade of a tree. Filtered sunshine."

"We have rules, Mr. Crenshaw," the principal growled. "Like no one leaves the building without signing out."

"Ah, Section 27(b)3 in the handbook, right? I could have sworn that said no one is to leave school *grounds* during the school day without signing out."

"No, it says 'the building.'"

"Are you sure? 27(b)3?"

"I have no idea the number. I know the rules." The principal pointed to his own chest.

Mr. Crenshaw scratched his head and muttered, "I thought I did too, but apparently not."

Danny thought the timing was right and he blurted out, "I can play today, right, Mr. Trufant?"

"Yes. Yes, of course." The principal looked disappointed that he had to go back on his own order, and he jabbed a finger in Mr. Crenshaw's direction. "But this can't happen again."

"No more nature therapy?" Mr. C raised his eyebrows as if that would be a terrible sin.

"Yes, I mean no, not no more, just no more leaving the

131

building without signing out. Understood?" The principal pushed his glasses up on his nose as he had begun to sweat.

"Oh, you scared me for a minute. I don't know a counselor worth his salt who doesn't apply a little nature therapy from time to time."

"You're not being cute with me, Mr. Crenshaw, are you?" asked Mr. Trufant.

"Not at all."

"Good, because I take rules very seriously in my building."

"We are on the same page, sir."

The principal turned to Danny. "I expect four or five touchdowns from you this afternoon."

Danny smiled big. "Yes, sir."

"Good." Mr. Trufant cleared his throat and glanced up at the second-story windows. "Let's take this show inside, now. There are people looking at us."

They followed him inside and separated at Mr. Crenshaw's office. When the door was closed, Danny thanked Mr. C. "He was gonna suspend me from playing, then he asks for five touchdowns."

"Sometimes, to do our job, we have to do things we don't want to do." Mr. C sat back down behind his desk.

"Like you spending first period with me," Danny said.

"That's my job, yes, but I enjoy it."

"Why?"

Mr. C shrugged. "I like to help people, kids especially. You're a good kid. I'd like to see you feel better."

"I feel fine."

Mr. Crenshaw looked like he was thinking. "Did you feel

fine when you dumped the Yahtzee box and ran out of here?"

"That was because . . ." Danny couldn't remember why he'd done that. He looked at the scattered contents of the game box and began to pick the dice up from the floor. He put the box back on the shelf. When he turned around, the counselor was looking at him, the question still fresh on his face.

Danny looked at the clock. "The bell's about to ring."

"Yes. I'll see you tomorrow?"

"Aren't you going to the game?" Danny asked.

"Would you like me to?"

"You could see why everyone is making a fuss over me."

"So being a good football player is what makes you special?"

Danny snorted. "It's Texas, right?"

The bell rang and Danny made for the door.

"So, I'll be impressed?" Mr. Crenshaw asked.

Danny didn't hesitate. "Yes, sir, you will."

Froston was one of three other junior high schools besides Crooked Creek that fed students into Jericho High, so the rivalry was a bitter one. Froston was also a town that looked down its nose at Crooked Creek because the average home there was twice as expensive and they had a mall in the town center with all the latest and greatest stores and restaurants.

Danny looked around the Crooked Creek stadium. That was something Froston didn't have, not like this anyway. The home stands held two thousand people. There was a press box and a concession stand with public bathrooms. It was as big as some high school stadiums—not Jericho's of course. But the people of Crooked Creek needed seats for everyone and the town had issued a bond five years ago to see to it, so this was a source of pride for all.

Danny stretched his legs and watched the Froston players

file off their bus in two columns. Their sky-blue helmets and jerseys seemed somehow overly proud to Danny. They took the field in perfect formation, and a slow, steady chant filled the air.

"We are . . . Frost-ton . . . We are . . . Frost-ton . . ."

They circled the entire field, sometimes passing within a few feet of the Crooked Creek players, before they emerged onto the field from the far goalposts. When they'd spread themselves evenly across the field, they began a wild rant of clapping and bellowing that ended with one final sudden clap that echoed off the brick side of the school.

Danny's teammates were on their backs, stretching their quads, when Cupcake erupted in a lone, loud voice that was obviously intended to be heard by their opponents. "Wow! That's some bad barley. They'd win the regional cheer competition, hands down!"

Danny and his teammates burst into nervous laughter.

"All right, Cupcake," Coach Kinen scolded as he walked among his ranks. "I hope you're this chipper after our first offensive drive."

"Just so long as you let the big dog eat, Coach, we'll all be chipper."

"Oh, and you're the big dog?" Coach Kinen asked.

"Not me, Coach. Danny Owens!" Cupcake hollered. "Feed the big dog and we'll send these rich kids and their baby blanket jerseys back where they belong."

As the team got to its feet for arm circles, they began to chant, "Dan-eee, Dan-eee, Dan-eee . . ."

They kept it up for the final few minutes of their stretching,

135

and Danny soaked it in. He couldn't help looking into the quickly filling stands, hoping his mom and Janey and even Mr. Crenshaw were there to hear. He found his mom and Janey easy because his mom wore his dad's black-and-gold number 33 jersey. They were on the fifty-yard line right below the press box. He didn't spot Mr. C.

Coach Kinen blew his whistle and stretching ended. Players lined up on the goal line and did agility drills back and forth until it was time for them to do some quick tackling drills and then run some plays. When the warm-up was complete, everyone surrounded Jace, barking and hopping up and down until the signal when they broke down into hit positions with a unified war cry.

They jogged to their sideline, where guys made last-minute equipment adjustments or got a final gulp of water before the national anthem and the coin toss. Jace won the toss, which prompted more "Dan-eee" chants.

Danny took a handoff up the middle on the first play. He hit the line like a cannonball. Bodies flew and tumbled. His legs got bogged down in the tangle of arms and legs, but not before he'd run for twelve yards and a first down. He hopped up, high-fiving his teammates and feeding on their excitement.

That's how they went down the field, Danny left, Danny right, Danny straight up the gut. His shortest run was seven yards and he punched it into the end zone from the fifteen-yard line, running right off Cupcake's big backside. The stadium— spilling fans from the stands—went crazy.

Cupcake's enormous head looked like it had been shoe-horned into his helmet. His eyes were bright as stars as he banged his facemask against Danny's. "This is just the beginning! It's all beef today! It's a *beef bonanza*!"

And it was.

Danny ran for 243 yards and scored five touchdowns by the fourth quarter, when the backup players went into the game to run out the clock. As he jogged off the field, the crowd stood up to cheer. Danny pumped a fist in the air. Coach Kinen gave him a hug and patted his helmet. Danny put his helmet on the bench and got a drink as teammates fist-bumped and high-fived him.

Up in the stands, his mom and Janey waved down at him, both of them beaming with pride. Danny felt his own cheeks flush with pride and he tried not to be obvious as he searched the crowd for his counselor.

He was glad, when he spotted Mr. C, that it didn't bother Danny to see him sitting beside Ms. Rait. It was a good thing, actually. He felt certain that after what they'd seen today, things would be very different.

After the game Danny's mom took him and Janey to the Pecos Diner on the edge of town. The gravel lot was filled with pickup trucks and SUVs, and as they entered, a wild applause broke out. When Luann, the owner, spotted them, her face brightened and she showed them right to a corner booth that had just been cleaned off. Luann wore her bleached-blonde hair stacked up high. She was a heavyset older woman with thick makeup and a deep southern accent.

"Everyone's talking about the game," she said, handing out menus. "I'm sorry I missed it. You're the touchdown king, right? Just like your dad, they're sayin'. Oh, I'm sorry, kiddo . . ."

Danny just pretended not to hear the last part and answered, "Thank you, ma'am."

"Five touchdowns." Danny's mom swept a hand across his hair.

"You sent those rich kids right back to where they came from. That's what I like." The owner splayed bright red fingernails across her chest. "You all have your supper and then I want each of you to have a piece of pie on the house. That's the least I can do."

"Thank you, ma'am."

"You might like the banana cream. I made that this mornin' myself."

"Yes, ma'am."

"And manners too." Luann raised her painted eyebrows before winking at Janey. "You hang on to this boy is what you do."

Janey blushed and cast her eyes on the menu. "Uh-huh."

"Shirley!" the owner yelled, drawing everyone's attention and startling a young waitress in a brown dress uniform. "You come take these folks' order. We got us a football star here. And bring a fresh bottle of ketchup."

Danny heard murmurs of approval around the diner and felt equal measures of pride and embarrassment. He kept his chin up, but he didn't look around at anyone. Their supper came promptly. Danny had a heaping plate of meatloaf and mashed potatoes smothered in gravy, which he quickly devoured. After the pie, his eyes began to droop.

"Now we'll get you home for a nice bath and a good night's sleep." His mom yawned herself. "You earned it."

"I wish," Danny said.

"Why's that?" his mom asked.

Danny pointed to the clock on the wall. "I got Ms. Rait at seven thirty."

"Don't fool with me, Danny."

"I do. Tell her, Janey."

Janey looked down again. "Yes, ma'am. He does."

Danny's mom sputtered and fumed. "I saw her at the game. You're exhausted. You played your heart out."

Danny had to admit that he was enjoying this. "She doesn't care. That's what she said."

"But not like that," Janey said. "She said it nice."

"Not to me," Danny said.

"You know, she's sitting right over there." Janey pointed toward the front. "I saw her and Mr. Crenshaw when we came in."

Danny secretly stole a glance and saw the back of Ms. Rait's head. "After she dropped you off at your house last night I swear she turned into a witch, said she didn't care about football."

"There's no cause to say that," Danny's mom said sharply. "I'll just talk to her on the way out. We'll get it fixed."

"I'm tellin' ya." Danny shook his head.

"She's new here." Danny's mom raised a piece of pie on her fork. "She saw you play, all those yards, everyone standing to clap when you came off the field, and in here too. I'm sure she gets it now."

She popped the pie into her mouth and gave him a wink.

Danny hoped it would be that easy, but he had serious doubts.

Danny's mom asked Shirley for the bill, but instead they got the owner. "Your bill's been paid, folks."

"Please, I insist." Danny's mom had her wallet out.

"You can argue with Mr. Colchester," Luann said, nodding her head toward an old farmer with glasses. She leaned close and lowered her voice. "He's loaded, so I'd just take it."

"Oh, Mr. Colchester." Danny's mom waved at the man. "Thank you, sir. That was unnecessary, but greatly appreciated."

"Saw your boy tonight. Crushed Froston! His father's son all right." The old man grinned, showing off a crooked set of teeth.

"Thank you, sir." Danny blushed and looked down at the tile floor.

He followed his mom blindly as they exited the restaurant

and ended up looking into Mr. Crenshaw's smiling face. Ms. Rait's crutch stood propped up against the booth. On the table sat two empty ice cream sundae dishes and two cups of coffee next to the bill. Danny smiled uncomfortably.

"Ms. Rait," his mom said, "you're just the person I wanted to see."

"Thank you," said the teacher.

"I saw you at the game," Danny's mom said.

"Yes." That was all Ms. Rait had to say, even though Danny's mom seemed to be waiting for more, maybe some praise for Danny's big game.

Danny's mom chuckled. "I think Coach Kinen thinks Danny is a plow horse or something, right? I mean, Danny left, Danny right, Danny, Danny, Danny."

"Yes, very exciting." Ms. Rait took a sip of her coffee.

"So, he's just worn completely out and I think the best thing is for him to get some rest, even though I know you two have plans. I'm sure you can make it up another time." Danny's mom grinned.

"No," Ms. Rait said, wagging her head, "we really can't. We have so much to do. I'm sure he can get through it, Mrs. Owens. He won't have to move a muscle."

"Look, I think what you're doing is wonderful," Danny's mom said, "and very kind, but Danny's just a kid, so I think this time it's more important that he gets some rest."

Ms. Rait took a deep breath. "Mrs. Owens? We had an agreement. I rushed here to scarf down dinner and I passed on a movie so I could work with Danny, so that's what I'm expecting to do. Making exceptions is what got him into this mess."

Danny's mom gasped. "You're questioning my judgment as a parent?"

"That's not what I said." Ms. Rait turned to Mr. Crenshaw for help, but he glanced at Danny and looked away.

"It's what you said without saying it." Danny's mom was getting loud. "It's what you *implied*."

People at the other tables turned their heads.

"Please don't raise your voice at me," Ms. Rait said softly. "I'm trying to help here."

Danny's mom frowned. "You're right. I know you mean well, but this isn't how things work."

"I agree." Ms. Rait slid out of the booth and was up on her crutch in one swift movement. She removed some money from the pocket of her jeans and put it on top of the bill.

"Oh, I've got that." Mr. Crenshaw quickly reached for his wallet.

Ms. Rait held up a hand. "Call me old fashioned, Bob, but I'm one of those people who likes to pull her own weight."

Ms. Rait started toward the door before she stopped and turned. "There are no free rides, Mrs. Owens. I hope you bring Danny at seven thirty."

Then she was gone.

Mr. Crenshaw flew after her without a word.

"Unbelievable." Danny's mom watched them go. "Well, Danny, you were right about her. Come on, kids."

Danny and Janey followed his mom. Janey's face was bright

red, and she kept her head down until they got in the car. Danny sat in front with his mom, and she looked at Janey in the rearview mirror as they pulled out of the parking lot. "I am sorry for all that, Janey. I never imagined she'd cause a scene. I don't like scenes, do I, Danny?"

"No, ma'am."

"No, I don't." His mom slowed as she approached the light in the center of town. She put on her blinker to turn.

"So, you're not going to take him to Ms. Rait's?" Janey asked in a quiet voice.

His mom made the turn and laughed, checking the mirror to catch Janey's eye. "That's funny. I like that."

Danny's mom put the radio on and no one said anything until they pulled into Janey's driveway.

"Thank you for dinner, Mrs. Owens, and the ride home, but I wasn't trying to be funny. I think Danny *should* go to Ms. Rait's. I think she's right about reading being important." Janey opened the car door and put one foot out. "I could even go with him again, if it would help."

Danny's mom twisted around. "Janey, that woman was downright rude."

"But she was right, and she believes in what she's saying." Janey spoke excitedly. "I don't think she meant to be rude."

Danny was tired and sore from the game. He wanted to do just what his mom said, take a long bath, maybe watch some TV, and then go to sleep, but something in the tone of Janey's voice made him think. And when he began to think, Mr. Crenshaw's reaction began to bother him. Mr. Crenshaw stood up for him against the principal, and he didn't hassle Danny for tossing the Yahtzee game or busting out of his office, either. Mr. Crenshaw was someone whose opinion Danny had to admit he cared about.

"Danny," his mom said, "I know you don't want to go . . . do you?"

And just like that, a decision that seemed quick and easy wasn't anymore.

"No," Danny said. "I don't *want* to."

"Good," said his mom.

Janey looked like she'd been slapped in the face, and it made Danny think again that maybe he was making a mistake, but he was worn out, and if his mom was happy . . .

"Don't worry, Janey. I'll do twice as much tomorrow."

"You think there'll be a tomorrow?" Janey asked. "You heard Ms. Rait."

"I'm sure that was her pride talking," Danny's mom said. "If she's for real, she's not going to punish Danny for something that's not his fault. Good night, Janey."

Janey got out of the car. "Good night, Mrs. Owens. Thanks again. See you tomorrow, Danny. Great game." Janey closed the door and left with a wave.

"Bye." Danny waved at Janey's sad face through the window. At home, Danny got directly into the bath.

"Can I get you a Pepsi?" his mom hollered from the kitchen.

"Yes, please!" Danny shouted through the bathroom door.

She brought in a cold can, holding a dish towel over her face.

Danny reached up and took it. "Got it, Mom. Thanks."

"Happy?" She kept the towel pressed tight to her eyes.

"It was a great way to start the season." Danny took a slug of soda and burped.

"Yes, it was." His mom felt for the door and backed out of the room. "I know you're gonna do it, Danny. You were just great, that's all.

"Hey, how about Mr. Colchester buying our dinner?" she added.

"And us getting a booth the minute we walk in?" Danny set the Pepsi can on the edge of the tub. "It's only the beginning, Mom. I'm gonna buy you a white Range Rover."

"White?"

"Yeah, you look good in white, Mom."

She laughed, making a light and airy sound. "Danny, I watched you today and it was like I was seeing your father. . . . You know he would've been so, so proud of you, don't you?"

"Shut up," Danny screamed. His heart pounding, he grabbed the can of soda and fired it at the tiled wall. The thin aluminum burst open like a grape, spraying the brown soda everywhere.

Danny's mom yelped and jumped back, dropping the towel.

"Mom, get out!" Danny bellowed. "Just get out!"

His mom backed into the hall, let out a gut-wrenching sob, and disappeared.

Danny sat in the tub, shaken to the core. When he realized the bathwater had become slimy and cold, he toweled off and attacked the mess in a businesslike manner. He cleaned the walls, floor, and mirror with a damp washcloth. Then he brushed his teeth and went straight to his room.

He turned the Xbox on and began to play *Siege* with strangers. Cupcake kept sending him invites, so he backed out and went into private mode so it looked to his friends like he'd gotten off-line. He found a group of four kids in Georgia and won several games with them before killing them all in the final round just as he'd done with his friends.

It felt good to kill them all, and he listened to them cursing him while he laughed gleefully, then shut down the Xbox. He lay on his bed with the lights on, staring at the airplane models hanging from their fishing lines. He wanted so badly to recapture the feeling he'd had after the game, when they'd cheered for him and when he walked into the diner, and especially when Mr. Colchester had bought their supper.

So he replayed the scenes in his mind, over and over, but instead of becoming clearer, the fog thickened. The harder he tried to regain the images and the feelings, the more distant they seemed. Finally, his thoughts turned to Ms. Rait's disapproval, Mr. Crenshaw's look, Janey's obvious disappointment, and his mother's pitiful sob. Those images trapped him like the tangle of sweaty sheets until he threw them off and jumped out of bed.

He dressed in sweatpants, a Steelers T-shirt, and sneakers before walking softly through the house. From the hall, he saw the light of his mother's bedroom TV flickering through the cracked open door. Canned laughter from some late-night comedy made a muted noise. He guessed she'd gone to sleep, but he was sure to be quiet as he slipped out the back door.

At first he didn't know where he was walking to, he just knew he needed to be out of bed, out of his house. After several minutes, he realized his feet were taking him to the creek. He dialed Janey but got no answer. Of course she was asleep.

He tramped along a cornfield, its bare stalks dry and rattling in a soft breeze. When he reached the woods, he used the flashlight on his phone to navigate the well-worn trail to the creek. He stopped and sat on a boulder beside the bank, and as he did, a half-moon emerged from behind a thick cloud. Soft white light danced across the broken stream. The light and the gurgling water made him think of a dream or some magical moment where an angel might appear to make everything right, but that didn't happen.

He crossed the stream and found their tree. Carefully, he climbed up, using a combination of branches and spikes to reach the fort they'd hidden from view, at least until the leaves fell. He was breathing hard by the time he got inside and lay down on the floor.

Danny sighed and curled up on his side in a ball. He couldn't help thinking about Bud in the story he'd been listening to, alone and cold and abandoned. That's how Danny felt. *Something* wasn't wrong; *everything* was. The moonlight suddenly disappeared. In the total darkness, he felt so alone and so miserable that he wanted to cry, but he didn't. He lay there with only the gentle rustle of leaves and the sound of his own breath for company, too sad and too empty even for tears.

An angry squirrel woke Danny.

Braced on all four feet as if it were ready to jump from the empty windowsill, it flashed its tail and chattered at him, baring its long yellow front teeth.

"Oh, scat!" Danny faked a lunge and the squirrel disappeared. "Stupid squirrel."

His body ached, his head too, partly from a poor sleep on the plywood floor and partly from the game against Froston. He flung open the trapdoor and swung his legs into the opening, feeling for the last spike with his toes. Going down was easier only because of the dawn sky glowing through the leaves.

A bird or two called out, but nothing so serious as in the springtime, when they seemed to sing for their lives. A chipmunk ran across the path, scattering sticks and leaves as it dashed for the safety of its nest. When he reached the stream, he scolded himself for crossing in the dark at night. He could have gotten hurt, and that would've wrecked his football season more surely than Ms. Rait.

By the time he got to his back door, the sky in the east glowed pink and he hoped his mom was asleep. Quietly he slipped inside, took off his shoes, and tiptoed toward his bedroom. He wondered what he'd been thinking when he left the house like that. Now he was tired and sore and jittery at the thought of being caught. He had no idea how mad his mom was about him yelling at her, but he knew she'd freak out if she realized he'd been away all night. He suspected the punishment would be extreme.

Danny breathed a sigh of relief when he set foot inside his bedroom. He'd almost closed the door when someone thrust a hand into the crack. The door bounced open, and there stood his mother with her arms crossed.

"Danny, where have you been?"

Danny's mouth sagged open. His stomach took a nosedive as his mom stared at him.

"I . . . took a walk." Danny told himself that wasn't a lie. "I was up really early. I heard some birds and I couldn't get back to sleep."

More truth.

His mom's eyebrows loosened up and her scowl began to fade into concern. "Danny, what's wrong?"

He shrugged. "What do you mean?"

Her eyes were like rays burning into him, but she spoke in little more than a whisper. "The soda can, yelling at me, up with the birds? You can talk to me, Danny. I'm your mother."

He had to look away. "No, I'm fine. Maybe you'll sign that paper and get me out of her class."

Now it was her turn to look away. "Let's see what she does.

If she's gonna play hardball with me, she's gonna lose, but she may come around. She's one of those people who're very proud of themselves. If she helps you, she'll be a star teacher. If she doesn't, she'll be a grouch with a big mouth. I think she knows that."

"I've got class with her third period." Danny was thrilled to be beyond the subject of his being out all night. "What should I do?"

"Let me make you some eggs," she said. "You'll just act like nothing happened. See what she says. I'm betting she asks you over to work on your reading after football practice."

"Can you make scrambled?"

"Of course."

"What if she doesn't say anything?" he asked.

"Call me. If she gives you the silent treatment, I'll talk to her. Now, get yourself ready and I'll make those eggs."

"With cheese?"

"Yes. Whatever you want, Danny." His mom flashed a smile and got to work.

After breakfast, he boarded the bus.

"Great game, Danny." Stephanie Stevens, a pretty eighth grader, held up a hand, which Danny high-fived.

"Yeah, Danny, awesome."

"Way to go, Danny!"

Then the whole bus erupted. "Dan-eee, Dan-eee, Dan-eee . . ."

Danny bit back a grin and grabbed a seat, saving one for Janey.

They picked her up and he whispered to her about how

everyone chanted his name before telling her about sleeping in the tree fort.

"Weren't you scared?" Janey's eyes got big.

"I didn't think about it. I was . . . I don't know, going crazy."

She looked him over and dusted a crumb off his shirt. "Well, you look pretty normal to me."

"I feel better now," Danny said. "But sometimes, I just lose it. I have no idea why. I just snap. I threw a Pepsi can against the wall in the bath. It blew up and I yelled at my mom."

He studied Janey's face. She looked like she was going to say something, then stopped.

"What?" he asked.

"Nothing."

"Aw, come on, Janey. It's me."

She looked him in the eyes. "You can talk to me, you know."

He let out a short laugh. "What do you think I'm doing right now?"

"About *anything*," she said.

The word "anything" hung between them.

"I know," Danny muttered as he dug into his backpack to get the Playaway. "I better listen to chapter four again. Maybe I can answer a question in Rait's class and get her off my back."

Janey looked again like she was going to say something, but this time he didn't want to hear it, so he quickly plugged the buds into his ears.

He liked the Playaway and the story. He paused it only for a moment as they entered school to say "see ya" to Janey. He decided to see just how serious Mr. Crenshaw was about him doing whatever he wanted, so he walked into the counselor's office with the earbuds in, said, "Hi," and sat down on the couch to listen.

Mr. C sat looking at him for only a few minutes before booting up his laptop and getting to work at his desk.

Later, Mr. C tapped his arm and Danny realized the bell had rung.

"Time, Danny. See you Monday. Have a good weekend."

Danny packed away his device. He couldn't help liking Mr. Crenshaw, an adult who actually did what he promised to do without trying any sneaky tricks to get Danny talking. "Are you going to the varsity game tonight?"

"You know, I hadn't thought about it. Maybe."

Danny laughed as he opened the door because who didn't think about going to the varsity game? Who didn't *go* to the varsity game? "Okay, maybe I'll see you there, Mr. C."

Math made Danny feel like a star football player again, so he was riding high when he walked into Ms. Rait's class. He stole a glance at her, but she was talking with Janey at her desk. Danny wondered if he was the subject of their talk, but neither of them looked his way, even when a couple kids who hadn't seen him yet called out their congratulations for putting five into the end zone against Froston.

He sat down and Janey came over and gave him a friendly fist bump before taking the desk in front of him like all was well.

Danny leaned forward to whisper. "Did she say anything about me?"

Janey turned around, surprised. "No, we were talking about our next reading assignment for class, and she said instead of getting too far ahead I should read *The Watsons Go to Birmingham*. It's another book by Christopher Paul Curtis."

"Oh." Danny couldn't help feeling disappointed, but he shook it off and followed Ms. Rait's diagram about plotlines and then the discussion about *Bud, Not Buddy*.

It was near the end of class when the teacher said, "So, everyone seems to relate to Bud, even though as I look around I'm guessing many of you don't share a lot of common experiences with the character. So what's the connection?"

Danny's hand went up at the same time he blurted out his answer without waiting to be called upon. "Grown-ups who say one thing and do another."

The class broke out in nervous laughter.

Ms. Rait held up her hands. "All right. All right. That's good, Danny. I'm sure many of you have had your parents say one thing and do another."

"And teachers," Danny said.

Only a few scattered bits of broken laughter were heard before a hush settled over the class. Danny stared at Ms. Rait, and she stared right back.

Danny reminded himself that he was a football star. He'd won a big game almost single-handedly, and everyone knew it. He tried to re-create the cheers from the game and the chants from the bus in his mind, but even that wasn't enough to keep him from dropping his eyes under Ms. Rait's iron look.

After class, Janey nudged him in the hall. "What was that about?"

"What?"

"*Teachers*?" She carried her books against her chest and narrowed her eyes at him.

He shrugged. "Just what I said. Teachers are grown-ups too. Sometimes they don't do what they say they'll do. She was gonna help me. Now she's not."

Janey took hold of his arm and stopped. People flowed past them like they were boulders in a stream. "You didn't do what she said. You didn't go to her house to work."

Danny rolled his eyes. "You should've heard everyone on the bus. Everyone knows what happened yesterday but her. She acts like it's no big deal, like football is nothing. Well, maybe it's nothing where she's from, but she's in Jericho County now. Even my mom is ready to stop playing around with her if she doesn't get into line."

"What's that mean?"

Danny tugged free and continued walking. "My mom said if Rait didn't talk to me about meeting today after practice, she was gonna call, but she told me to give her one last chance."

"Danny," Janey said, catching up, "I'm your best friend, but I think you've got this backward."

The first bell rang and they'd reached the point where they had to part ways.

"Gotta go, but I'll see you at lunch." Danny marched away, secretly taking out his phone in the crowd to call his mom like she'd asked. Just before he walked into his next class, he ducked into the bathroom and dialed.

When his mom answered, he said, "She gave me the silent treatment."

"Don't you worry," his mom said. "I got this."

Danny's smile lasted until lunch. Cupcake was already working on a meatloaf sandwich when Danny sat across from him, his tray loaded down by four tacos, two apples, and three milks.

Cupcake peered at the tacos. "Bro, just looking at those makes me need to go to the bathroom, and you got four? Can't see you makin' it through practice, but I guess you pop it into the zone five times your life is pretty much all beef, huh?"

Danny took a big crunchy bite of a taco. "I'm a running back, so I've got a much stronger constitution than a lineman."

Cupcake wrinkled his brow. "What does a boat have to do with your stomach?"

"Cupcake, the constitution I'm talking about is the stuff you're made of, your toughness. You're thinking of the USS

Constitution—one of the first ships built for the US Navy. If anything could make me switch from model war planes to model boats, it would be her."

"Sounds like the same thing, kinda." Cupcake filled his mouth with meatloaf and bread, nodding to himself at his own wisdom.

Janey arrived and sat down next to Cupcake and opposite Danny.

"What's the same?" she asked.

"Model airplanes and model boats." Cupcake spoke through his food.

Janey looked up briefly as if thinking. "Yeah, I see that."

"Ha!" Cupcake pointed at Danny, grinning, until some chewed meatloaf appeared between his teeth.

"Aww, yuck." Danny waved his hand and turned his head away.

"Tough to be wrong when you're the star of the team, but that's life on the farm."

When Janey and Danny didn't say anything, Cupcake looked back and forth between them and formed an opinion. "Wait, what's going on with you two? Something's wrong."

"A minor disagreement," Danny said.

"Major." Janey fired a dirty look at Danny before taking a container of peaches and cottage cheese out of her lunch bag and digging in with a plastic spoon.

Cupcake listened to Danny's side of the story, then said, "Rait better watch her step. If she knows what's good for her, she'll do what your mom wants."

"I doubt she will," Danny said. "In fact, I know she won't."

"Why should Ms. Rait watch her step?" Janey asked Cupcake.

"Because my bro here owns this town after yesterday. The guys on the team already said they'd run her out of town if she messes with their franchise."

Janey's mouth fell open. "It was a junior high football game, Cupcake."

"Tell that to the people." Cupcake spread his arms and raised his hands, looking all around them like a satisfied king.

That made Danny laugh. Janey dismissed them both by returning to her lunch.

Danny took another bite of his taco, thinking it needed something. "When she says she's done helping me, my mom's gonna do what she shoulda done from the start: switch me out of Rait's class."

Janey kept her head down but shook it from side to side to signal how she felt.

"Oh, come on, Janey." The taco was a bit bland, so Danny drizzled some hot sauce on it. "You're being way too serious."

The flecks of gold in Janey's brown eyes seemed to glow as she looked up at him. "I hope I am being too serious. I hope you never need Ms. Rait, Danny. I hope you never look back and regret not working with her . . . but I'm afraid you will."

Danny's phone buzzed during sports study hall. He was in the library playing penny hockey with Cupcake across a table. He disappeared into the back corner of the reference section and called his mom back.

"So, what'd she say?" Danny whispered.

"Don't even get me started." His mom spoke so loud he glanced around.

"Shh. I'm in the library."

"Oh. We can talk when you get home." His mom crunched something in her mouth. "But you'll be in a new class by tomorrow morning. I can tell you that."

"Okay, thanks, Mom. Gotta go."

Danny hung up and pumped his fist in the air. He went back to the table where Cupcake sat twisting a paper clip into a rabbit's head. Danny reached into his backpack and fished out the sheet of sight words he was supposed to be learning. Carefully, he folded it into a paper airplane. He aimed and let it fly.

Clunk.

It was a direct hit into the metal wastepaper can.

"Nice shot," Cupcake said. "What was it?"

"I guess you could say it was Ms. Rait getting put in her place." Danny laughed and Cupcake followed along like the good friend he was.

Later, when he and Cupcake walked into the locker room together, his teammates began the "Dan-eee" chant as they banged their palms against the lockers. Cupcake raised Danny's hand like a fight champion and everyone cheered.

Danny bit the inside of his mouth, trying hard to keep his smile from becoming too proud. He changed like the rest of his teammates into shorts and a jersey. He put on his football cleats and grabbed his helmet. When he turned from his locker, Bug was blocking his path.

"Dude. Bonfire. Tomorrow." Bug spoke in grunts. "You in?"

"Uh, yeah. Can Cupcake come too?"

Bug narrowed his eyes. "Cupcake's a hog."

"And that's a good thing?" Danny knew "hog" was a football term that meant lineman, but in Crooked Creek it might mean an actual hog, as in a pig.

"Hogs are automatically invited." Bug turned and marched away.

"Ooo-kay," Danny said under his breath, thinking that he'd have to go but that he'd ask Cupcake first.

The older players said the day after a game was always a

very light practice that would end with some running to flush the soreness out of their legs. The air was festive out on the practice field during stretching, even though the sky was dark and hinting at rain. Laughter rang out amid wisecracks and tomfoolery. Even the coaches' eyes weren't as squinty as normal. When Coach Kinen blew his whistle, though, the team gathered around a stern face.

"Danny Owens? Where are you, Danny?" Coach Kinen searched around.

Danny hesitated because this wasn't the tone he'd expected from his head coach. Ms. Rait flashed through his mind. He couldn't help thinking that she had something to do with the scowl on his coach's face.

Danny swallowed, stepped forward, and raised his hand.

"Do you want to practice today, Owens?" Coach Kinen stared coldly at Danny.

"Yes, sir." Danny couldn't imagine why his coach was asking such a question.

"You *sure* about that? You sure you're *happy* here?"

"Yes. Sir."

No one said a word. Danny felt the sweat beading on his upper lip.

Coach Kinen broke into a grin. "Cuz your agent called me this morning looking for more money."

Coach Kinen tilted his head back and howled at his own joke. Everyone joined in, even Danny, who felt a flood of relief.

"All right. All right." Coach Kinen raised his hands for quiet. "That was a nice win and a nice way to start the season, but we travel to Westfall next week, and they've got a line that averages two hundred twenty pounds on both sides of the ball, so we've got our work cut out for us. Okay, let's line it up for agilities."

Coach let fly a short, sharp blast on his whistle and practice began. They mostly made adjustments based on things that hadn't gone as planned in the opener and walked through some new plays. During the offensive team period, Coach Kinen surprised everyone when the second-string offense went in.

Danny's backup was an eighth-grade speedster named Scott Port. Scott had done a nice job replacing Danny late in the game the day before, so no one expected him to be replaced.

"Port, stay with me." Coach Kinen pointed to the ground in front of him. "Markle! You've been begging to go on offense long enough. Show me you can carry the ball—take halfback."

If Danny hadn't had such a fantastic game the day before, he would have been upset to see Markle put in a position where he'd now compete for Danny's playing time.

"You're fine, Port," Coach said loudly enough for the whole team to hear. "A little light in the pants for a line this big, though. We're going to be grinding it out, and if Danny needs a breather I want some bulk in there. That's Markle."

"Got it, Coach." Markle beamed with pride.

The second-string offense walked through the same set of plays as the starters, only Markle added sound effects to his performance. First, he'd make explosion sounds as he hit the line. Then, on the way back to the huddle, he'd imitate the roar of the crowd before and after announcing that he'd scored another touchdown.

"And Markle does it again! Another seventy-yard touch-down run for the kid from Crooked Creek!" Markle raised both hands high as he marched to the huddle.

Everyone got some laughs out of it, even Danny.

After the backup offense had gone through about twenty plays, it was time to run some 110-yard conditioning sprints simply called "110s" to end practice. Spirits were still high, and Danny's teammates continued to rib him about his imaginary "agent" and a new contract.

"You gotta get your agent to cut out these 110s," said Jace as they lined up.

"I know he wants to sign *you* up," Danny said, "so you should just make that part of the deal."

"Oh, no," Jace said. "I'm not the one going varsity as an eighth grader."

Danny couldn't even reply, he was so flustered and flattered by the team captain's compliment.

"Okay, you daisies, stop complaining and line up!" Coach Willard yelled at them while Coach Kinen stood at the other end of the field with his stopwatch to make sure they ran their sprints in under twenty seconds.

The whole team lined up across the back of the end zone.

Coach Willard cupped his hands around a thick gray walrus mustache. "Set, go!"

They took off running. Once they passed Coach Kinen, they peeled off to the closest of the two sidelines and jogged back to Coach Willard, where they lined up to do it all over again.

Ten times they had to sprint the length of the field. It was grueling. After the first five, all the linemen were given an extra five seconds to make it, but even that was brutal for guys like Cupcake. On the last sprint, it was a tradition for the players to race. It was something Danny always won, and even though he'd had the big game the day before, he wanted to prove to the coaches that he wasn't done working hard to get better.

His legs ached and his lungs burned, but he coiled his muscles in a sprinter's stance and shot forward on Coach Willard's start. This last sprint was more about heart than speed because everyone was gassed. From the corner of his eye, Danny saw Port and Markle surge ahead. The two of them were racing for pride—Port to show he was faster than Markle and Markle to prove he was tougher than Port, and both to show they were better than Danny.

He had to beat them both. A kid who'd be going to varsity as an eighth grader had to dominate his teammates. He dug deep, forcing his limbs to swing faster despite being numb. The burn torched his lungs, but he kept on, closing the gap and taking the lead in the final ten yards.

When his foot hit the goal line first, he immediately backed his weight to slow down fast. His feet slapped the ground until a sharp pain pierced the side of his right foot. This pain was white hot, like a bolt of electricity.

Danny stumbled. In the instant before he crashed to the turf, he wondered if he'd stepped on a nail, so deep and so fundamental was the pain.

When he hit, he saw stars and felt another sharp pain in his shoulder, but neither one concerned him because he knew that something serious had happened to his foot.

Coach Kinen appeared above Danny. "Okay, stop screwing around, Danny."

"Oh, oh, oh!" Danny squeezed his leg below the knee, rolling on his side in pain. "Coach, my foot."

"Are you kidding me, Owens?"

"Coach, I'm *not*." Danny winced and gritted his teeth. He couldn't believe the pain. It made no sense.

"What did you *do*?" Coach Kinen knelt down beside him.

"Nothing. I was running. It felt like someone stabbed my foot, or like I stepped on a nail." Danny had his ankle in both hands.

Coach Kinen looked at his cleated foot. "I don't see anything."

Suddenly Danny swallowed hard. Bile churned up from his stomach. He was scared, scared enough to make himself sick.

"What is it, Coach?"

"Here, let's try to get you up." Coach Kinen put his hands under Danny's arms and lifted.

Danny stood on one leg and tentatively placed his right foot on the ground. As soon as it touched he snapped it back into the air because it felt like he'd stepped on the same nail, maybe worse this time.

"Did you twist it?" Coach Willard asked. "Is it your ankle?"

"It's my foot." Danny's voice broke and he bit down on his mouthpiece. "I can't walk."

"Foot?" Coach Willard looked at Coach Kinen, who shrugged.

"I have no idea," the head coach said. "Let's get his mom to take him to Doc Severs. You call her and I'll get him up to the locker room."

Coach Willard took out his phone and Danny told him his mom's number while Cupcake and Coach Kinen each slipped a head under one of Danny's arms. The rest of the team fell in behind them, keeping respectfully quiet. Danny had no idea what had happened, but the pain told him that whatever it was, it wasn't a minor injury. As hard as he fought it, the pain and the fear made his eyes watery. He sniffed and kept his head down, thankful for the helmet and the cover it gave him.

There was a bench outside the locker room, and that's where they set him with his leg up. Coach Kinen removed Danny's shoe, which hurt enough that Danny couldn't help grunting with pain even though he clamped down tight on his mouth guard.

"Mom's on her way." Coach Willard held up his phone as he marched past.

Coach Kinen and Cupcake stayed with Danny, even as his other teammates began to filter out of the locker room with their street clothes on. Cupcake's brother, Herman, pulled up in his pickup and got out to investigate. Cupcake filled him in with a hushed voice.

Herman put a strong hand on Danny's shoulder. "I bet you're gonna be fine, Danny. Can't be anything too serious, right?"

"Right," Danny said weakly.

Ten minutes later, Danny's mom pulled up along the curb and stopped with a screech before jumping out of the car. "Danny, what in the world?"

"I don't know." Danny shook his head.

"I texted Doc Severs at the health center," Coach Kinen told Danny's mom. "He's the best. Just give your name at the desk and he'll take you in right away."

"Thank you, Coach."

"Here, let's get him in the car." Cupcake helped Coach Kinen as Danny limped between them.

He got loaded into the front seat. Coach Kinen tossed his cleated shoe in the back and patted the roof. "Okay, Danny. Good luck. We need you, kid. If we're gonna win a championship, we surely need you. Let me know what they say."

40

He closed the door and off they went, with his mom chattering about how she was sure it couldn't be serious. Between sentences, she took long drags on the unlit cigarette in her hand—her way of getting ready to quit smoking entirely.

"I mean," she said, looking over at him for what must have been the tenth time as they pulled into the front circle of the medical center, "you can't hurt yourself bad just running, right?"

She left him in the car and ran in to the desk, taking out her insurance card. It was only minutes before a nurse came out with a wheelchair. She and his mom helped Danny into a wheelchair and took him right into the X-ray room.

"Dr. Severs wants a few pictures," she said.

"He was running sprints," Danny's mom said. "You can't break something just by running, right?"

The nurse gave Danny's mom a patient smile. "It's standard procedure to get some X-rays. Let's get him up on this table."

They helped Danny up out of the chair and he scooted his butt back onto a raised table. The nurse put a lead apron around his torso, and then a radiology technician slipped a flat, black X-ray cartridge under his foot. Everyone left the room. There was a short buzz and the tech came back with another cartridge, changing the angle of his foot. He took four pictures in all before Danny got back into the chair and was wheeled into an exam room to wait.

His mom continued to fuss. "I can't believe it's anything, Danny. Are you sure you can't walk? I mean, should you try again?"

"Mom, my foot is killing me." He looked at her in disbelief. Did she think he was faking an injury? He could feel a steady throb of pain on the outside edge of his foot.

"Maybe I tore a ligament. I don't know. It just . . . went snap, and I went down." Danny clutched his ankle as if to cut off the pain.

Dr. Severs entered the room with the X-rays under his arm. He was a tall, lean man in a white lab coat. He had a large head and wore stylish black-rimmed glasses. "Hi, Danny, Mrs. Owens, I'm Dr. Severs. Let's see what we've got here."

The doctor slipped an X-ray up into a clip on the top of a light box hanging on the wall. "Hmm."

Danny could see the ghostly white image of his ankle and the puzzle pieces of his twenty-six foot bones.

The doctor yanked the X-ray and snapped another one into its place. "Hmm."

He examined all four before turning to Danny. "Let's take a look at that foot."

"Did you see anything, Doctor?" Danny's mom wrung her hands.

"Not yet," he said coolly.

The doctor took Danny's right foot gently in his hands and looked closely at Danny's face. The long fingers crept around his foot.

"That hurt?" asked the doctor as he went. "That?"

"No," Danny said over and over as the hands moved closer to the spot where the pain was like a police siren.

When Dr. Severs touched the spot on the outside edge of Danny's foot halfway to his heel, Danny yelped and jumped.

"Okay," said the doctor. "That could be a couple things. Let's get you an MRI."

Dr. Severs had the door open and was on his way out when Danny's mom asked, "What things? Nothing serious, right, Doctor?"

The doctor paused. His face gave nothing away. "I really can't say. We'll get the MRI and I'll know more."

"But nothing that can't heal . . ." Danny's mom let the words hang out there.

"I don't want to worry you unnecessarily," said the doctor, "but I can't say it isn't serious until I know what we're dealing with here."

They went down the hall to where a large white MRI tube stood in the middle of a spacious room. Danny was put in the tube, and the tech left the room. The MRI machine was loud and seemed to take forever, but finally they finished and wheeled him back into the exam room.

Danny's mom was a wreck. He smelled cigarette smoke on her and figured she was too upset to be calmed by imaginary smoke. That made him more nervous, because he felt the same way she did. How could it be anything super serious when all he had done was run some sprints?

Finally, Dr. Severs reappeared. If his face was any indication, it wasn't good, but reading his face might mean nothing. The doctor sat down on the stool beside the exam table and looked up at them. "Okay, here's what we've got."

"There's a tiny hairline stress fracture in the fifth metatarsal. It didn't show up on the X-ray, but we got it on the MRI." The doctor looked back and forth between Danny and his mom.

"He got this just by running?"

The doctor nodded at Danny's mom. "Yes. He may have weakened it in the game yesterday, but these small fractures usually present with something as seemingly harmless as running."

"So, it's small," Danny's mom said. "That's good, right?"

"These things usually heal up in six to eight weeks with rest," the doctor said.

Danny's mom brightened. "Six weeks! So you'll be back for the big game, Danny. Maybe a few weeks before. You'll be rested for the last part of the season. We'll make lemonade out of lemons."

"Okay, so that would be the best-case scenario," the doctor said. "Let's not count on six weeks, though, because everyone is different."

"Even eight weeks won't be the end of the world." Danny's mom was almost silly with joy. "The championship's in nine. It's part of Danny's grand plan."

"I know about the game, but the issue with this type of injury is rest. He's got to keep the weight off the foot until it's healed."

The doctor wrapped Danny's foot in a compression bandage. He took a deep breath and looked at Danny sternly while talking to his mother. "If he doesn't keep off that foot and follow the RICE protocol, he may never fully recover."

Danny felt his stomach plunge. The paper on the exam table crinkled beneath his weight as he squirmed.

Danny's mom furrowed her brow. "Rice? What rice?"

"The nurse will explain." The doctor patted Danny's leg and stood up. "The lemonade is that even in the worst-case scenario, he *will* be able to walk."

Danny's mom put a hand on the doctor's arm to keep him from going. "Walk? Not run?"

"If it doesn't heal—but I expect it will; more times than not it does—but if it *doesn't* heal, then running would just be too painful. We'll get you some crutches, Danny, and you really need to stay off the foot completely for the next five weeks. You can do some light leg machines in a week to keep your tone. We'll get another MRI in five weeks and see where we're at. Hopefully you'll walk out of here."

The doctor looked at them with a forced smile. He seemed

eager to get away. "Okay, you can make an appointment at the desk. Come back in five weeks. And I can't say it enough, stay off that foot."

As soon as the doctor had gone and closed the door, Danny's mom began to weep. She put her arms around his shoulders and hugged him to her.

"Oh, Danny," she moaned.

"Mom, I'm okay. It's gonna be fine." Danny wriggled free just as the nurse came into the room with the crutches.

The nurse explained that RICE meant rest, ice, compression from the wrapping, and elevation. She adjusted the crutches to fit Danny. His mom pretended to study a chart with a gruesome drawing of a knee and all its inner parts as the nurse showed Danny how to use the crutches.

"Now, these are going to make you sore under your arms at first," the nurse told Danny, "but you'll get used to them. You may start to feel better soon, but please remember you need to keep all your weight off this foot until the doctor clears you."

She gave him instructions about icing his foot often for the next two weeks.

"Yes, ma'am, I got it." Danny made himself sound cheerful as he swung himself toward the door. "Come on, Mom. Thank you, ma'am. See you in five weeks."

Danny's mom spoke in a low, pained voice to the woman at the desk who made the appointments. Danny was the one who accepted the paper appointment card from her and thanked her. They got in the car and his mom began crying again, just softly this time. Danny turned his head to the window and hunkered down for the long ride home.

When they finally did get home, his mom sat at the kitchen table and put her head down into her folded arms.

"Mom, you gotta stop. It's gonna be fine." Danny could barely speak, he choked so on his words.

She held her head up and looked at him with dark, tear-stained makeup running down her cheeks. "That's just what your father said. Every time. You . . . you just sounded so much like him. . . ."

Danny's face went still. His heart felt like it had exploded in his chest, and rage began to boil up into his brain.

"Shut up!" he screamed, and it was as if it was someone else was screaming. "Shut up! Shut up! Shut up!"

He swung his crutch like a flipper. The lamp on the stand next to the couch shattered. The light bulb popped in a blue flash.

"Danny!" his mother yelled. Danny got down the hall and into his room before striking the door with the same crutch. It slammed shut as his mom screamed again at him from the kitchen. "You come back here! Daniel, you come back here this instant!"

He heard her loud and clear and he shouted through the door, "No!"

Danny locked his door and then put his Xbox headphones on and turned up the volume. He thought he heard his mom knocking, but it stopped after a while. He didn't know why he couldn't talk to her, just that he couldn't. With the Xbox settings on private, he would be able to tell when his friends got back from the varsity game, but if they got online they'd have no idea he was even signed in.

He played and played, cursing people he didn't know, killing opponents in the game with earnestness. He grew tired before he did his trick of dispatching his own team and shutting down the game. He got up, balanced on his crutches, and pressed an ear to his door. He heard the TV in his mother's bedroom, so he snuck out and quietly crutched into the kitchen.

It wasn't easy, but he found an empty plastic grocery bag and filled it with some leftover pieces of chicken from the refrigerator, ice, and a can of soda. He quietly used the bathroom before retreating to his room. After slamming down the chicken and soda, he iced his foot, then tied up the garbage in the bag and went to sleep.

In the morning, he woke to the sound of gentle knocking.

"Danny?" His mom spoke softly. "Danny, honey?"

Danny held his breath. He felt terrible about the night before. His foot hurt, but his heart hurt more.

"Yeah, Mom?"

"Can I make you breakfast?"

"Yeah, Mom."

"Oh good. I'll make scrambled with cheese like you like."

"Okay. Thanks, Mom."

Danny used his crutches to get into the bathroom. Balancing on one, he brushed his teeth and changed into fresh clothes.

"You look nice," his mom said as he entered the kitchen.

"Thank you." Danny kept his voice and his head down, feeling ashamed of the way he'd behaved the night before. He still didn't know why he had acted that way.

"How's your foot?" She was trying to sound upbeat, even bubbly.

"Sore."

"Let's ice it." His mom got an ice pack from the freezer.

Danny nodded and sat down at the table and propped his foot on a chair with the ice. He remained silent until she brought his eggs. "Thank you."

"Of course." She sat down across from him with a strong-smelling mug of coffee. "So, we both kinda lost it last night, and we don't have to go there, but I've been thinking and I'm determined to see a couple things through."

Danny took a small bite and chewed.

"You're hearing me, right?"

"Yes, ma'am." Still, he couldn't look at her.

"Good. So first, I'm going into school with you Monday morning to talk to Mr. Crenshaw. I don't know why you're doing some things that you've never done before, but I need to know if I can help. Honestly, right now I feel like I'm part of the problem."

"You're not." Danny met eyes with her briefly before hanging his head again and filling his mouth with eggs.

"Well, I want to see what he has to say, and . . ."

Danny could feel her eyes on him, and she didn't speak until he finally looked up.

"I want to apologize to you," she said.

"No, Mom. It's my fault." His lips felt numb.

She shook her head. "I'm your mother. God knows I should have learned something about all this by now."

She sighed before continuing. "You're just so good, I got caught up in it, the cheers, the looks, Mr. Colchester buying our dinner. It's exciting, but I know better than anyone you can't build your whole life around a game. Or . . . you shouldn't, anyway."

She looked right at him. "We need—*you* need—to act like football doesn't even exist, because it might not."

"I'm gonna get better." Danny gritted his teeth.

"I think you will, too." She nodded enthusiastically. "But if you don't, or if something else happens, it's my job to make sure you're okay, that you have other things you can do."

"Like what?" Danny had never considered doing anything other than the NFL.

"Oh, Danny, there are hundreds of things . . . you could be a doctor, or a lawyer, or an engineer. Think how smart you are in math."

"Mom, I'm stupid in school." He swallowed because it hurt to say. "I can't read."

His mother stared at him for a moment. "Exactly."

"Exactly what?" he asked.

"You can't read well," she said softly, "but you will."

43

Danny would have argued with his mom about going into school early Monday morning to see Ms. Rait and talk to Mr. Crenshaw, but he was still horrified by the way he'd behaved Friday night. He considered himself lucky that his mom hadn't taken away his phone and his Xbox and grounded him for a month for telling her to shut up. He spent the weekend doing the ice treatment and being quiet and as helpful as he could on crutches. Cupcake called, all excited about the bonfire, promising Danny would love it as soon as he could go. On Monday morning, he went along quietly, bracing himself for the embarrassment that was sure to come.

"I texted Ms. Rait." His mom backed the car out of the garage.

Danny sat beside her with the crutches wedged between him and the car door. "What did you say?"

"I apologized." She checked both ways before pulling out of their driveway. "Profusely. That means 'a lot.' Then I asked if she'd meet with us."

"And what did she say?"

"Fine," she said, punching the air with her unlit cigarette. She used it like a drum majorette with a baton. "Fine!"

"That's it?"

"That's all I need." His mom gave a short nod. "Humble pie. I've had it before. Nothing wrong with it. Works on even the hardest cases, and Ms. Rait's not a hard case."

"She had me fooled," Danny said. Ms. Rait reminded him of his Pop Warner coach, Coach Hitchcock, who'd been a sergeant in the Marines.

"We'll see."

It was strange being at the school early. The teachers' parking lot was only half-full, and the hallways were empty and quiet. Many classrooms they passed were still dark, but Ms. Rait sat at her desk and waved them in.

When she saw Danny's crutches, her eyes widened for a moment. She regained the blank look on her face before she said, "Please sit down."

Danny and his mom took the two desks closest to the teacher. Danny felt embarrassed for his mom, sitting there in a middle school desk, but she smiled warmly. "Thank you so much for agreeing to sit down with us, Ms. Rait."

"That's not a problem." Ms. Rait had her dark hair pulled back tight, and it made her look older and sterner. "What is a problem is seeking exceptions to the rules, so if you're here for that, this will be a very short meeting."

Danny's mom dipped her head, shaking it sadly before she looked up. "No, that's not why we are here. We are here to apologize in person, both of us, and to politely ask you for a second chance. No strings. No exceptions."

Ms. Rait pursed her lips. "I assume this has something to do with your crutches?"

Danny looked at the floor, his cheeks hot.

His mom spoke clearly. "Yes. You're absolutely correct. That's what it took. Yes, I got caught up in the hype. Then Danny got hurt, just running. He should be fine, but we don't know that, and it reminded me of the end of my husband's career. They thought he'd be fine too, but he wasn't."

The room went silent.

Danny tuned out his mom's comment and looked at a poster on the wall showing Taylor Swift with a stack of books. Something about reading, he guessed.

Finally, Danny's mom spoke again. "They say those who don't learn from history are doomed to repeat it. We will abide by all your rules, without question. We just humbly ask you to forgive us and give us another chance."

Ms. Rait blinked at them. She took a deep breath and nodded to herself. She sat silently in thought. It seemed forever . . . before she finally spoke.

"This back-and-forth . . . it's no good," Ms. Rait started. "I can't teach unless I have a plan. I execute the plan. I stick to the plan. You're in, then you're out, now you're suddenly in again." Ms. Rait threw her hands up in the air. "This is really it, folks. I won't go back a third time."

Danny's mom stared at Ms. Rait. The silence became uncomfortable.

Danny's mom cleared her throat. "So you'll do it? You'll teach Danny to read?"

"Yes, that's what I said."

Danny's mom popped out of her seat. She was beside the desk clasping one of Ms. Rait's hands in two of her own. "I wasn't sure what you were saying, but Ms. Rait, you won't regret this. Danny is going to be the best student you ever had. I mean the best at being the hardest working. I know he has a lot to learn, but he will. Oh, he will."

Danny's mom pumped the teacher's hand until Ms. Rait blushed. "All right. Good. Can you get to my house around five thirty?"

"He'll go straight from practice," Danny's mom said.

"Practice?" Ms. Rait said. "He's hurt."

"Injured guys have to watch," Danny muttered.

"Oh. Well, I'll be happy to take him home afterward," Ms. Rait said.

Danny's mom held up her hand. "No such thing. I'll get him when you're done. You're doing more than enough. Thank you. Danny, thank Ms. Rait."

"Thank you, ma'am." Danny kept his head and voice low from embarrassment.

"I'll see you in class, Danny."

They left and walked back through the school toward the front offices.

"That went well." His mom mussed the top of his hair.

"We'll see." He was thinking about Mr. Crenshaw. He saw a red plastic fire alarm on the wall and considered pulling it to avoid the meeting. He thought that might be some kind of a crime, though, and wondered if, when you pulled the handle, it sprayed invisible ink on your hand that the police could see.

Before he could come up with a better plan, his mom knocked on the counselor's door. Mr. Crenshaw opened the door to greet them, then showed them to the couch before he pulled up a chair facing them. He pointed at the crutches. "I heard you hurt your leg."

"Foot." Danny raised his foot slightly.

"Sorry, foot. But I heard you'll be back for the big game."

"That's the plan." Danny fell silent.

Mr. Crenshaw turned his attention to Danny's mom. "How are you today?"

She sat on the edge of the couch with her hands folded in her lap. "Well, we had a very nice meeting with Ms. Rait, so, so far, so good."

"I'm glad to hear that. I'm also glad you came to see me. I like Danny a lot. He's a great kid."

"Yes. He is. I know he's our only child, but I can't imagine a better one."

"That's so nice to hear." Mr. Crenshaw sounded for real, but all this cheerleading made Danny uncomfortable because he felt something else was just around the bend.

"But . . . well, sometimes, lately, he isn't quite himself," Danny's mom said.

"Can you tell me what you mean?" The counselor acted like he knew nothing, which annoyed Danny.

"Well, he's here in the first place because he fought with the Markle boy." His mom shrugged as if pounding some kid's face in was a standard way to start out the school year. "But there's been things with me, too. Yelling. Slamming doors. He broke a lamp. It's just not like him."

Mr. Crenshaw raised an eyebrow. "Danny?"

Danny shrugged and looked at his crutches.

"Is your mom right?"

"Yes, sir."

"Do you want to talk about it?"

Danny looked at the counselor's kind face. There was no

judgment in it, and unlike most adults, Danny didn't feel like he had to answer a certain way to keep him happy.

Danny shook his head.

Mr. Crenshaw nodded that it was fine. He turned to Danny's mom. "I don't want to push him."

"How can he get better if you don't push him?" Danny's mom sounded a bit impatient.

"Mrs. Owens, Danny has had a lot of things happen to him recently." Mr. Crenshaw spoke with soft kindness. "When people experience traumatic events, their heart can kind of freeze, to protect itself, make it hard. That can—and usually does—change how a person acts."

He paused to see if Danny's mom was following him. She patted Danny's knee.

"Now, you love him and you'd like to see him back to the way he was before his heart froze, so to speak. And my job is to help." Mr. Crenshaw leaned forward in his chair. "But I don't want to use a hammer and chisel, because when you break ice that way, you can break what's inside it as well. Think of me as a heat lamp. I want to melt the ice slowly, and when it's safe to do so, Danny will tell us what's wrong. We just have to be here for him, listening and warming him and keeping him as safe as we can. Does this make sense?"

"That's all you want me to do?" she asked. "Just be there? No coaching?"

"Right. Just be there. It seems like you've been very understanding so far. Danny's lucky to have a mom like you."

"Oh—" She waved him off.

"It's true. Many parents aren't as understanding," Mr. Crenshaw said.

"Well." His mom looked at her finger and twisted her wedding ring, then stood up and shook Mr. Crenshaw's hand. "Thank you."

Danny spent the day thinking about his frozen heart when he wasn't thinking about schoolwork. Even on crutches he got to Ms. Rait's class with time to spare and sat down behind Janey. She didn't speak to him, but she didn't give him a nasty look either, so he started things off.

He sighed loudly. "Well, you can say 'I told you so.'"

She turned around with a frustrated look. "That's not what I wanted to say. You didn't call me all weekend."

He smiled. "Phone works both ways, you know."

She hung her head for a moment. "I thought you were already mad, then Cupcake told me about your foot and I figured I was the last person you wanted to hear from."

The bell rang and they had to catch up in the hallway and at lunch. By the end of the day, things were back to normal between them, and that felt good to Danny. He was actually feeling upbeat as he crutched into the locker room. He used the bathroom, and since he was in no hurry because he couldn't practice, he was fixing his hair in the mirror after washing his hands when someone spoke behind him.

"Hey. Owens."

Danny turned and was surprised to see Markle standing there with all his gear on minus his helmet.

"Guess what?" It was Markle's nasty tone that seemed so

out of place. It was as if they hadn't buried the hatchet less than a week ago.

"What?" Danny asked automatically.

"You hurt your little footy?"

"It's a stress fracture." Danny scowled.

"Yeah, whatever." Markle glanced over his shoulder to make sure they were alone before he said, "Just know this: you might as well not even worry about coming back."

"What are you talking about? Why?"

"Because we don't need you. We've got a new running back now." Markle smiled that arrogant, mean smile Danny thought he'd seen the last of. *"Me."*

Football practice was never easy. Danny could remember moments with his face in the steaming grass, sweating and struggling to get those last push-ups, or the burning in his legs from running sprints until he was dizzy and sick. In those moments, Danny recalled longing for relief from the heat and the grind, a seat on the bench, a mouthful of cool water, a patch of shade.

Now, he had all that—his dreams come true—but he was miserable. There were no "Dan-eee, Dan-eee" chants. No one even said his name. They didn't look his way. They were getting ready for the Westfall game and the opposing team's massive line. All eyes were on Markle, and Markle wasn't disappointing them. He ran mean, like his words of betrayal to Danny. It was betrayal, to have pretended to make peace in front of Jace and the rest of the team while secretly resenting Danny, even hating him.

"Markle!" Coach Kinen's shout had an edge that brightened Danny's spirits and he eagerly looked up from the blade of grass he'd been knotting to watch the spanking Coach Kinen's voice seemed to promise.

Coach Kinen stomped toward Markle as the player jogged back toward the huddle. "What's your read on that play?"

Danny snickered to himself and shifted his leg and the ice bag to allow his foot a more comfortable position on the bench.

The confused look on Markle's face was priceless. "The free safety?"

"Yes!" Coach Kinen hugged Markle to him, slapping the back of his helmet. "Yes, the free safety. You ran the crossing route and drew him away, and *that's* why Carmody was wide open on the post. Touchdown, gentlemen, because everyone does his job. And Markle's only been back at running back for a couple days, but he knows his assignments."

Coach Kinen looked over at Coach Willard. "I love this kid, Coach Willard."

Coach Willard looked like a mountain in the middle of them all. "As you should, Coach. As you should."

Danny's delight turned to nausea.

He clenched his teeth and wondered how he could expose Markle for the selfish, backstabbing jerk he really was.

When the team finished practice with sprints, Danny was jealous. He never thought he'd miss sprints, but he did. He'd rather suffer along with his team than work leg machines or sit there with his leg elevated and an ice bag on his foot, feeling less than useless. When Coach called the team together, Danny got up and used his crutches to get to the middle of the field. Coach Kinen didn't even wait for him to get there. He missed half of the speech, but he got there in time to hear Coach Kinen praise Markle again.

"If we can do like Markle, all of us, raise our game, answer the call when we're needed most, we will not only win this game, we will win the *big* game, the championship.

"All right, bring it in, men. 'Championship' on three. One, two, three . . ."

"CHAMPIONSHIP!"

Danny remained quiet.

The team broke apart and headed to the locker room. Danny lagged behind. The two coaches who'd stopped for a private meeting caught up to him halfway to the school.

"Danny. How's that foot feeling?" Coach Kinen sounded like he'd only now even noticed Danny was alive.

"Pretty sore." Danny tried to strike a tone somewhere between pain and toughness, but felt like a wimp.

"Yeah, it'll take some time, but you'll be back. Dr. Severs thinks so." The coach shucked a stick of peppermint gum before folding it into his mouth and giving Danny a quick pat on the back. Then both coaches surged past him to continue their discussion.

Danny paused to rest his armpits and watch them go. He strained to hear anything they might be saying about him until it hit him that they just didn't care.

It happened that fast.

One injury, and he was no longer the darling of Crooked Creek. He wasn't Dan-eee, Dan-eee, Dan-eee.

He was just Danny Owens.

Cupcake came out of the school, saw Danny, and broke into a grin. Cupcake walked over to him, put his arm around Danny's back, and gave him a squeeze. "Bro, you don't know how lucky you were to miss those sprints."

Danny tried to explain to his best friend that he'd been thinking the same thing and why it just wasn't true. Cupcake gave him a knowing smile. "Aw, c'mon. Stop kidding me. Hey, there's my brother. Let's go."

Cupcake helped Danny up into Herman's truck and then handed in his crutches before circling around to the other side where he got into the passenger front seat.

"How's the foot, Danny?" Herman looked at him in the rearview mirror.

"Pretty sore." Danny liked the way that sounded now, better than when he'd answered his coach.

"Yeah. I bet." Herman put the truck in gear and held up his left hand. "Had one of those myself once. Hairline fracture in my hand. Nothin' they could do, so I taped it up, took some Advil, and just kept milkin' the cows."

Danny was horrified that he somehow looked soft. "I think it's different with your foot."

Cupcake glared at his brother. "Yeah, it's different with your foot. You can't even walk if it's your foot. Right, Danny?"

"That's what the doctor told me." Danny felt a wave of gratitude for Cupcake. "He said stay off it for five weeks until he sees me or I might mess it up and not be able to run again."

"Herman. He's Danny Owens. He's headed to the NFL. We're not talking about milking cows."

Herman glanced at his brother. "Milkin' cows put that shirt on your back, you little turd."

"I'm not saying anything bad about milking cows. I'm just saying that Danny is on a different program. His arms and legs and feet, those are his cows."

"Yeah, I guess." Herman sulked until they got into town. "Hey, you guys want an ice cream?"

"Sorry, I can't. I gotta get right to Ms. Rait's. Would you mind dropping me there first, Herman?"

"Sure thing." Herman went straight through the light, past the houses in town, drove another half mile, and pulled into Ms. Rait's driveway. "Hey, Danny. I didn't mean nothin' bad about the tape and me keepin' on workin'. I was just makin' small talk is all."

"No, I know." Danny slid out of the back door and slipped on his backpack before steadying himself on the crutches.

"Thanks for the ride, Herman. Thanks, Cupcake."

Cupcake seemed pleased that the air was clear. "Hey, let's get online later and kill some zombies, huh? I'll ask Janey, too."

"Sounds good." Danny shut the door and watched them drive off in a cloud of dust. When he turned toward the house, he came face-to-face with Mrs. McGillicuddy.

"Well, hello."

The cat gave a yowl and then wove in and out of his legs, purring insistently.

"I'd pick you up," Danny said looking down at the cat, "but I'm handicapped."

"That word is offensive."

Danny looked up to see Ms. Rait standing on the porch looking down at him. His face felt hot. "I . . . I didn't know that. I'm sorry. I thought they have handicapped parking, so . . ."

Ms. Rait didn't seem angry. "Yes. I call it 'accessible parking.' That's what it is, don't you think?"

Danny thought about it for a minute. "Yes. I do."

"In England, the term 'disabled' isn't considered offensive, but I don't like that either because I'm quite able." Ms. Rait seemed almost happy to talk about it. "I think of myself as 'using a crutch' even though I'll probably always use it, whereas you'll hang them on your garage wall in a few weeks." She paused, then said, "Well, come on. We have a lot to do."

Ms. Rait held the door for Danny, which embarrassed him, so he tried to move quickly. "Thank you, ma'am."

Mrs. McGillicuddy scooted inside before Danny with her belly swaying.

In the kitchen, there were two glasses of iced tea on the

table along with a stack of papers. Mrs. McGillicuddy waited beneath Danny's chair, her puffy white tail swishing like a feather duster.

"Sit right down."

Danny leaned his crutches against the wall and did as he was told. Ms. Rait sat across from him and reached down into the book bag at her feet. She pulled out a paper airplane and slid it across the table at him. Danny had a sinking feeling as he unfolded it to see the word list.

"I . . . uh . . ."

She smiled at him. "That's okay. You didn't need it then, did you?"

"I didn't think so," he said quietly, reaching down to scratch Mrs. McGillicuddy's ears.

"Librarians always cover their English teachers' backs." She sipped her tea and then set it down with a thump. "Ready?"

"Yes, ma'am." Danny smoothed the paper.

"From the top." She pointed at the sheet of sight words, then pushed a piece of scrap paper and a pencil across the table. "The ones you don't know, I'll tell you, and you'll write them out five times."

They launched right into it. She pushed him like a coach, demanding and no-nonsense. His brain felt like a sneaker in the clothes dryer: spinning, turning, thumping, and finally heating up. He looked at the clock, then at the word she was pointing to.

"I . . ." He shook his head and winced. "I don't know. I can't."

"Yes you do, and you *can*." She raised her voice ever so slightly.

He clenched his teeth and pounded a fist on the table, rattling a spoon and the top to the sugar bowl. "How can you say that? You don't know what I know."

She sat back and crossed her arms. "Is that what you say to Coach Kinen when he tells you to get him five yards? You *can't*?"

"You're not—"

"Not what?" She raised an eyebrow. "Not a coach? Let me tell you something. I'm the most important coach you'll ever have."

She pointed to the sheet of words again. "You know 'all,' and we went through all the variants: 'tall,' 'wall,' 'call,' 'fall,' and 'ball.'"

"Yeah, I know." Danny stared at the word until his vision got cloudy.

"And you learned 'moon,' 'soon,' 'goon,' and 'noon' because they all have o-o-n, which makes the 'oon' sound. Now, this is the core of your problem, and we are going to beat that problem, but I need you to do this. Put those two things together. Look at that word: b-a-l-l is what?"

"Ball?"

"Yes! Now keep going. Add the o-o-n sound to it." She was as excited as a football coach, he had to give her that.

"Ball-oon."

"Say it fast!" She nodded vigorously.

"Ball-oon, bal-loon, balloon!" A light went on. He jumped

up out of his seat and raised his arm and spiked an imaginary football, as if he'd just scored a touchdown. "Balloon! Haha!"

"That's reading, Danny! *You're reading!*"

Danny sat back down and Mrs. McGillicuddy jumped up into his lap with a yowl and they laughed together.

"Balloon" was only the beginning. It was like your first time running for a first down—a big moment that quickly got lost in the need for more and bigger and better and then ultimately putting it over the goal line.

After five weeks of mind-bending work, a dozen sheets of sight words, and repetition that made the endless football drills Danny had done throughout his life seem brief, he read a book. It wasn't much of a book. It was *Miss Daisy Is Crazy!* It was a kid's book, with pictures, but it was a book that he read and enjoyed on his own.

So, as he sat in the medical center waiting room to get the word on his foot, he distracted himself by reading the second book in the series.

"Danny, come on." His mom stood over him, impatient. "They called your name."

He wasn't sure if he'd missed when they called his name because he was scared to death or because of how goofy the book was. He handed it to his mom and gathered his crutches. He didn't think he needed them, but even if he hadn't taken the doctor's orders seriously, his mother had never let up on her insistence that he stay off his foot.

They followed the nurse into the MRI room, where he spent what seemed like days in the MRI "space capsule" with the huge magnets spinning inside their plastic skin. The constant thumping and banging cut into the headset they gave him, spoiling the country music he tried listening to. Finally, he was done and they deposited him in an exam room where his mother was waiting.

"Well?" She looked at him expectantly.

"Mom, I have no idea."

"I just didn't know if you overheard anyone saying anything." She bit her lip and frowned at the door, which opened as if on cue.

"How is it?" his mom asked the doctor before he could say a thing.

"Let's take a look." The doctor grinned at her and took Danny's foot in his hands.

Danny bit into his tongue so he wouldn't wince. He was ready to lie, if that meant getting back into action. He had to get back. Markle had run for his second hundred-yard game yesterday, and people were beginning to talk about how anyone with some talent could run behind such a talented offensive line.

The doctor began gently running his fingers along the outside edge of Danny's foot. "That hurt?"

"No."

"Hmm." Dr. Severs gave the bone a squeeze.

"It feels fine, Dr. Severs." Danny was surprised. "Really."

"Really?" The doctor gave the bone another squeeze as he studied Danny's face.

Danny held his breath and didn't move a muscle. Again, it was okay. It didn't hurt. "Yes, sir."

The doctor finally released Danny's foot. "Well, the MRI looks good. It seems to have healed nicely. Let's see how a week without crutches goes. No problems after that and I'll clear you to practice. If that goes well, you'll be back in action in two weeks."

"Two weeks?" Danny felt like throwing up. "The season . . ."

"The season goes for three more weeks. Crooked Creek is undefeated, and the toughest games are behind you. You may be able to play in the championship. But you still need to take it easy." The doctor thumped Danny on the back. "Now, look, you have to tell me if this starts to hurt. I know all about the big game and why you want to play in it, but you have to think long term. You don't want to do anything that could jeopardize your ability to play sports at all, right?"

"No, sir." Danny couldn't look him in the eye.

"Good. Very good. It starts to hurt and you get right back on the crutches and get in here." The doctor tapped some notes into his laptop and then spoke to Danny's mom.

"Did you get Danny the pair of wooden-soled sandals I recommended, Mrs. Owens?"

"Well, Doctor, the shoe salesman said these Birkenstocks were much better than the sandals you recommended."

Dr. Severs laughed and said, "They are better . . . and much more expensive." He had Danny put them on and stand for inspection, then said, "They're great! You can make an appointment at the desk for next week. See you then."

Danny automatically reached for his crutches, then stopped. "So I can walk without the crutches?"

"Yes, but take them so that if you need them, you'll have them. Right?" The doctor paused at the door.

"Okay."

"Great. See you in a week." Dr. Severs vanished, leaving the door open.

"I'm so happy for you, Danny." His mom gave him a hug and took the crutches.

Danny gave the crutches one last look and tried to look confident walking out.

49

Danny felt nervous sending his first-ever text. Not being able to read had limited him to phone calls, so his friends ragged him for being "old school." He sent it to Janey and she replied right away, "U bet!"

"Mom, can you drop me off at the guardrail by our fort?"

She gave him a disappointed look. "I thought we were going to the game together."

"We can, but that's later. I just haven't been to the creek since the crutches and it's been so hot today, I thought I'd go for a swim."

She slowed down and Danny got out.

"We'll have dinner at six," his mom said. "Invite Janey if you like. She can come to the game with us."

"Okay." Danny closed the door and watched her leave. He walked carefully on the uneven ground. If he was going to play

208

football in two weeks—the thought of waiting that long made his throat tight—he had to watch his step.

The air was so humid that even the shade provided little relief from the heat. He got to their fort and heard a chattering sound above. A squirrel was sitting on the windowsill, looking down at him and flashing its tail.

"Hey." Janey appeared, startling him.

The squirrel continued to scold him until Janey picked up a smooth rock and fired it. The stone struck the sill, and the squirrel disappeared inside the tree fort with a harsh squeak. Another rock clattered off the plywood walls, and Danny saw the squirrel racing up the tree for cover.

"You okay?" Janey asked. "What did the doctor say?"

"All good! Another two weeks and he'll let me play."

"Great! I knew you'd do it!" Janey poked his arm. "I can't believe you texted me. Welcome to the twenty-first century."

"Yeah, well . . ."

Janey giggled.

"What's funny?" Danny paused in the middle of the path.

Janey held up her phone and showed him his text.

"What?"

"Well, I'm not making fun of you because I know 'fort' isn't one of your sight words," she said.

"Yeah, so I sounded it out."

She laughed. "I know, but you typed 'fart.' 'Meet me at tree fart.'"

Danny laughed at that too. "I'll remember it now." He wiped the sweat off his forehead. "Could it be hotter? Let's take a dip."

Danny's worries multiplied as they kept walking. When they reached their water sluice tubs, Janey asked, "So, you're feeling good?"

"Sort of," Danny said. "But even if I can play in the big game, I think Markle's gonna have my spot."

She stared at him for a minute, and her brown eyes seemed to change colors in the dappled sunlight filtering down through the trees. Her words were as gentle as the breeze. "You don't have to play varsity as an eighth grader to make it to the NFL."

"Yes, I do!" Danny shouted. He took deep breaths to calm down. "That's how it works, Janey. I need to make varsity next year, get my feet wet, start as a freshman, all-league as a sophomore, then all-state as a junior and I'm a five-star recruit. Then, I go to a school where they play me, start me, I make all-conference, all-American, and I'm a high-round NFL draft pick. It's like stacking blocks. You have to have the foundation to build the tower tall. The foundation is now. Like my dad said, this is the year."

He choked up, and he turned away to strip down into his boxers and ease into his water sluice tub. The tub's bearded edges were bright green and soft with algae. The creek water was cool and clear. Gradually the fire in his brain cooled.

Thick clouds rolled in over the stadium on the back of a stiff breeze. The Friday night lights already burned bright over twelve thousand fans for the varsity game, most of them wearing Jericho Cowboys' gold and black. The visitors, whose stands only allowed for two thousand of the twelve, wore orange and white. Jericho took the field and the crowd roared with applause.

It deafened and delighted Danny and his two friends. His mom gave him a knowing smile as well. This was Friday night football in Jericho County. Even the long walk through acres of parked cars wasn't bothering him like he had feared it might, and that cheered him.

Danny thought it was like strolling down the midway at the state fair. People with cowboy costumes and painted faces lined the way. Grills sizzled and smoked between parked cars and trucks, and the hiss of beer and soda cans being opened was everywhere. Laughter, music, banners, and balloons were everywhere too. Danny ached for the party to be in his honor, for *his* team, and it made him more determined than ever to play in the big game.

The junior high championship wouldn't be a sold-out crowd like it was now for a Friday night varsity game, but there might be as many as seven thousand. That's how many had gone to last year's county title game. A win for Crooked Creek this year could put him on the Jericho varsity—on his way to being part of the Friday night spectacle next year. The thought gave Danny chills.

As the Cowboys did their thing down on the field—a slow, steady grind, running the ball, chewing up time, and playing a vicious brand of defense—Danny cheered along with the rest of Jericho County. But, unlike most, he felt connected to the players. The crowd's energy charged him.

When Jericho scored their second touchdown with a ten-yard run up the middle, Danny raised his own hands and slowly rotated around, soaking up the cheers and smiles around him. He found himself thinking about the permanence of Friday nights in Jericho, how this was the present, but he was the future. That led him to the past, when his father tore up the field with his moves.

As memories of his dad began darting through his head, and the roar of the crowd became deafening, Danny suddenly lunged for the aisle, pushing Janey and Cupcake out of his way.

"Danny?"

He heard his mom cry out behind him, but he was already

halfway down the bleachers when her words registered in his brain. He hit the bottom of the steps and split the middle of a teenage couple to double back on the stairs leading to the concessions. He jumped the last three steps, sprinted around the corner, and slapped both hands across his mouth as he rushed into the men's room.

The urinals were full and he wasn't going to make it to the stalls. He turned toward the sinks. Before he could quite get there, a spray of vomit blasted through his fingers, coating the mirror and two sinks with a brown-and-yellow spatter.

"Aww!" A chorus broke out around him.

Another wave of nausea rocked Danny's stomach and he heaved again, this time hitting the bowl of the sink. Still, it spattered all around.

"That is disgusting!"

"What's wrong with you, kid!"

"Aw, what a mess!"

"Gross!"

Danny spun around and kicked a stall door, crying out in pain. The door slammed inward, then banged back at him. His foot throbbed. Danny cursed and headed for the exit. People scattered to avoid his smell—or maybe it was his rage they feared.

A boy just a bit smaller than Danny bumped into him. Danny thought he recognized him from somewhere, but he gave the kid a shove anyway and kept going toward a grassy spot beside the concession stand. He staggered and doubled over, choking and gagging although nothing came up. His eyes watered, and deep inside his nose the stomach acid burned.

"Hey!"

Danny turned and saw five kids in a half circle, fists dangling by their sides.

"What's your problem?" the biggest kid said.

Danny peered through the shadows and stumbled back.

It was Markle.

51

"I'm sick, okay." Danny hated the sound of his own voice. It was . . . weak.

"I'm sick." Markle mocked him with a high-pitched, whining voice. The circle of Markle's gang grew tighter.

Then, out of the shadows, Janey appeared, her voice rough and tough. "Hold it right there!"

Markle froze, startled until he realized it was Janey.

Markle laughed. "You here to rescue your boyfriend? He needs it."

Markle's gang laughed. They were a rough-looking bunch. None of them were on the football team. They were all scrawny and ragged, kids who smoked cigarettes in the woods behind the school.

"You can say what you want," Janey said, "but you're gonna

look awful silly with half your teeth knocked out."

Things got quiet.

Markle straightened his back and sneered. "How 'bout I pull that ponytail and see how loud you squeal?"

That got his buddies loose and laughing again.

"How about not?"

Markle's legs buckled. He went down on his knees and Danny saw Cupcake standing behind Markle with a massive hand wrapped around Markle's neck.

"What?" Markle cringed and twisted his head around. "Let go, Cupcake. What are you doing?"

"What are *you* doing?" Cupcake rumbled like a diesel tractor going uphill.

"I'm just messing around." Markle pawed at Cupcake's hand. "C'mon, let me go."

Markle's last three words were desperate and high pitched, not unlike the tone he'd mocked Danny for. His buddies edged away instead of forward.

"Danny?" Cupcake asked.

"Ask Janey," Danny said.

"Janey?" Cupcake raised his eyebrows.

Janey glared. "You can do whatever you want with him. I'm not afraid of him."

Cupcake shook Markle's neck and his head wagged back and forth. "Well, we're teammates, right? So, I'm gonna let you go, but you better remember about the team thing too, Markle. Danny's your teammate."

Cupcake thrust Markle away from him. Markle massaged his throat and coughed a few times. "You coulda killed me."

"That's right." Cupcake folded his arms and stood his ground. "I coulda. Remember that before you think about getting cute with my friends next time."

Markle grumbled but faded away with his gang.

"Thanks, Cupcake," Danny said.

"Yeah, you did good." Janey tossed her head and her ponytail flew from side to side. "What was that? Some special jujitsu choke hold?"

"Nah." Cupcake shrugged. "Just a farmer's grip."

The stands above erupted with screams of joy and cheers and clapping. Jericho had scored its third touchdown.

"What happened, Danny?" Janey asked. "One minute you're cheering with us, the next you're running away."

"I got sick." He looked down. "Some of it got on me."

"Was it something you ate?" Cupcake narrowed his eyes.

"I don't know. Maybe. I just—all of a sudden—got sick."

Danny's mom appeared with worry all over her face. "Danny?"

"Hey, Mom. Sorry, I just . . . got sick. I barely made it to the bathroom and I got some on me." He looked down at his soiled shirt.

"Oh, Danny. Let's get you home," his mom said.

"I don't want to ruin the night for you all," he replied.

"I can get a ride with my brother," Cupcake said. "He drove my mom and dad. Janey, you can come with us."

"That's all right," Janey said. "This'll probably be a blowout anyway."

"Yeah, but those are the best ones." Cupcake glanced in the direction of the field.

Janey laughed. "I'm good. I had it covered, but thanks again, Cupcake."

"Anytime." With a smile and a wave, Cupcake disappeared.

"Had what covered?" Danny's mom asked.

"Um, just finding Danny. I had it."

"I got sick all over the place in the bathroom." Danny looked in the direction of the men's room and saw some unhappy faces on their way out. Some held their noses. "So I wanted to get out of there, but then I got sick, and then I saw this grass, so . . ."

"And I . . . just followed my nose," Janey said.

Danny's mom waved a hand in front of her own face. "I got it. Whew! C'mon, Danny. Let's get you home and into the shower."

They rode with the windows down and Danny in the back seat. Janey gave him a worried look when she got out in her driveway. He watched her walk toward the front door without looking back. Her parents didn't go to football games. Her dad was in dental sales and traveled most of the time, and her mom had to watch Janey's two-year-old twin sisters.

Danny's mom pulled into their own driveway and got the hose from under the deck. "Let's get those clothes off before you walk through the door."

Danny stripped to his boxers and headed inside as she sprayed down his clothes in the grass. As he showered, Danny tried to remember what had made him so sick. He remembered cheering for Jericho and then stumbling into the bathroom and the mess and the embarrassment and Markle. He finished and dried off, then dressed and found his mom in the living room.

"Hi." She muted the TV. "Better?"

"Yeah. Lots."

"Good." She tilted her head. "What do you think happened? Those pork chops I made for dinner were fresh, I know that."

Danny sighed and shook his head. "I'm tired."

"Get some sleep. Give your mom a kiss first."

Danny kissed her.

As he lay awake in his bed, he worried about many things. Football. Markle. Janey. Reading. Ms. Rait's exam. Also, Mr. Crenshaw.

Lately, the counselor had been probing Danny's mind. Where he'd once let Danny be, he now asked a lot of questions. Somehow Danny just knew his getting sick was going to come up. Mr. Crenshaw had a way of getting inside his head, and last week Danny had given up trying to fool him. There was something comforting about telling things to Mr. C. He listened. He nodded. He said kind things in a quiet voice that made Danny feel better.

The thing about him getting sick was that Danny had a pretty big feeling it was important. Mr. C was going to sniff it out and ask him. He knew he'd answer, and he couldn't help feeling that, come Monday morning when that happened, it was going to change everything.

"So, how was your weekend?" Mr. Crenshaw jumped two of Danny's checkers with his only king.

"Yesterday, I cleaned the garage and hung out with Janey and Cupcake at the tree fort. Saturday, I watched practice. Bored out of my mind."

Mr. C tapped the board to remind Danny it was his move. "That leaves Friday night."

Danny shrugged and began a retreat with one of his two kings.

"That means something happened." Mr. C made a move to cut off Danny's retreat.

Danny sighed. "Here we go."

"Here we go what? Am I going to beat you?" Mr. C pointed at the board.

"No. You. Inside my head." Danny looked him in the eyes

and realized for the first time what a deep blue they were.

Mr. C smiled. "That's my job. So, what happened?"

Danny looked at his hands. "I lost it. Bonkers."

"Bonkers how? Can you tell me what you did?"

Danny moved a checker to protect his king. "It wasn't like usual, me shouting or hitting something. It was like . . . inside. I got sick. My guts twisted. I ran to the bathroom. Puked everywhere. I don't know why. I was just watching the game. We scored and I puked."

Mr. C moved, keeping the pressure on Danny's king. "Do you remember what you were thinking? When they scored?"

Danny reached for a piece, then paused. "About how I'd be out there one day. That Jericho football is this thing that's bigger than . . . I don't know, bigger than life."

"Why would you say that?"

"Well, you've got the present, and I'm the future, and the past. It's, like, eternal, right?"

Mr. C's voice got soft. "Tell me about the past. What does Jericho football in the past make you think of?"

Danny moved his king into the open. He kept his finger on the piece for several moments. He knew this time was coming. It was like a long line for a water slide. It took so long it seemed you'd never get there. Then, there you were, in the tube. Then you let go. It was dark and you didn't know how it would end, but it was too late to go back.

"Tell me," Mr. C said gently. "What?"

Finally, Danny took his finger off the king and looked up at Mr. Crenshaw with tears flooding his eyes. His face twisted and his voice broke. "My dad."

"Yes," Mr. Crenshaw said, nodding the way you'd greet a long-awaited guest, "your dad."

A primal howl boiled up from Danny's center. He tilted his head toward the ceiling and let it out, sobbing and moaning in complete anguish. "I hate him! I hate him!"

Danny pushed back his chair and stood up. "Mr. C, why did he do it? Why?"

Mr. C stood up and circled the table, still speaking softly. "Do what, Danny? What did he do?"

"He died! He died, and I killed him . . ." Danny threw his arms around the counselor and sobbed into his shoulder. "I killed him. He was training *me*. He wanted me to be ready for the big game. He wanted me to have a great season and he took me running and if he hadn't done that, he wouldn't be . . . dead."

"Oh, Danny." Mr. Crenshaw hugged him. "You didn't kill him . . ."

"I did. I *did.*"

"No, Danny. No."

"He . . ." Danny sobbed. "He just fell and I watched and I couldn't do anything. I just *stood* there!"

"There was nothing to do, Danny. Your dad was gone. It's not your fault. He loved you and he wanted to help you, but it wasn't your fault. You have to believe me." Mr. C had Danny in a vise grip.

Danny cried until he ran out of tears. Mr. C got him a box of tissues. He blew his nose and sat back down. "I'm sorry."

"For what?"

Danny pointed at the stack of used Kleenex.

"It's good to cry, Danny. You kept that in for a long time. Too long."

"What do you mean?" Danny kept his eyes on the board.

"Did you cry at your dad's funeral?"

"No!" All he remembered were the people, all the people, and his mom in a black dress. He looked up so Mr. C would know it was the truth.

"Did you cry another time? Late at night? Before you went to sleep? Taking a walk in the woods?" Mr. C looked at him doubtfully.

Danny let loose a tattered sigh. "I guess not."

"That's why this is good. You needed it. You might need more of it. Don't be upset if you find yourself crying. It's normal. It's how we heal." Mr. C spoke with such confidence and authority that Danny believed him, and it made him feel much better.

Danny sniffed and pointed at the board. "It's your move."

"Oh. Right." Mr. C jumped the king Danny had had his finger on for so long and smiled weakly. "Sorry. You can't win them all."

"No." Danny kept his smile in check. "You can't."

In the hallway after English, Janey asked him about his puffy eyes. Danny told her his allergies were acting up.

"Oh," she said, and then she waved the review packet Ms. Rait had given them in the air. "How are you coming with Ms. Rait? You got all this down?"

Danny frowned. "I don't know. She said it's gonna be close. I swear though, it's like there's this little part of her that's still hung up on me missing a few days back in the beginning."

"Well, I'm sure you'll be fine. You're texting like a fiend."

"That's easy. I've read books, too. Only chapter books, but still." Danny shrugged. "Anyway, she said she's gonna give me a practice test to take. Then, we'll know."

"I can help you study." Janey smiled apologetically. "We spent half the day yesterday at the creek when we probably should have been studying."

He waved a hand. "I can't study all the time. I think I heard somewhere that's not good for you."

"From who? Cupcake?"

"Probably."

They both laughed.

"This weekend, we'll study," Danny said. "Next weekend, maybe we'll go to the bonfire."

"What bonfire?" she asked.

Danny told her about Bug and how Cupcake said the bonfire was great.

"I've seen that kid." Janey stopped where she'd peel off to her next class. "He's scary."

"Yeah. All the guys go, though. Think about it."

"Okay. See you at lunch."

That afternoon at football practice Danny felt like he was losing his mind. Markle ran for his third touchdown in a live goal-line period, and he exploded up from the pile of bodies in the end zone.

"Yeah! Yeah! Yeah!" Markle screamed, his ugly face red and contorted behind the facemask, his fists clenched. "That's what I'm talkin' about! Let the big dog eat!"

When Markle did that thing where he pretended to be spooning food into his mouth from an imaginary bowl, Danny had to turn away. He couldn't block out the sounds of his teammates joining the fray with Markle, though.

"Yeah, Markle!"

"Yeah!"

"Go Big Dog!"

"Yeah!"

"Eat!"

Unfortunately for Danny, turning away meant he also heard Coach Willard talking with Coach Kinen.

"Wow. Kid can carry the rock, Coach," Coach Willard muttered to Coach Kinen. "Where'd we find him?"

Coach Kinen shook his head in disbelief. "He was here all along. Right under our noses. He didn't run anything like this in camp. Sure stepped up his game though."

Coach Willard turned toward the huddle to give the offense the next play. Danny looked away quickly and kicked at the turf with his toe.

"Danny," Coach Kinen barked. "Come here."

Danny looked up and tried to read Coach Kinen's face as he approached. It told him nothing. When he got close enough, Coach Kinen put an arm around Danny's shoulder and turned him away from the action.

"How's that foot?"

"Hundred percent, Coach." Danny put as much positive energy into his voice as he could.

"Really?"

"Yes, sir."

"Cuz you look like you're favoring the other foot to me." Coach Kinen's look penetrated Danny's soul.

Danny blinked. "I don't think so."

"Hmm." Coach Kinen stopped and turned them both around so they could watch Markle burst through the line, break to the outside, and snag a bullet pass from Jace for another touchdown. The players went crazy.

Coach Kinen scratched his leathery neck. "Well, I'm not sure if it makes sense to rush back and take a chance that it's still not healed."

Danny's stomach heaved. He tasted vomit burning the back of his throat but swallowed it down. "But Coach. You said . . ."

Coach Kinen looked at him in the unfriendly way coaches look when being questioned by a player. "I said what?"

Danny's tongue froze.

He didn't know what to say.

"You said . . ." Danny swallowed again, then raised his chin.

"Yeah?" It was a challenge.

"Coach, you said you needed me to win a championship." Danny tried to stop the tremble of his lips by biting down hard on the bottom one.

Coach Kinen looked off in the distance for a moment before he said, "Football's a funny sport, Danny. It's a lot like life. Things change. Things happen that you don't expect."

The coach peered at Danny. "I'm thinking of you. I mean, does it make sense to rush back and risk making it worse, when . . ."

The offense ran their play. Pads popped like a gunshot. Markle stood over the linebacker he'd flattened and let out a battle cry.

"Wooooo! You do not take on Markle! Not 'less you want a mouthful of shoulder pad! Chump!"

Coach Kinen looked from the knot of players swarming Markle back to Danny. "When you might not even play, Danny."

Coach Kinen wore a pained expression. "I can't just stick you back into the starting lineup. Markle has played too well, and we're on a roll."

"I'm not asking you to stick me back in, Coach. I'll earn my job back. I just need a chance." Danny tried to sound strong and confident, and he thought he was doing a pretty good job.

"You're a seventh grader, Danny. You've got all next year," Coach Kinen said.

"Coach, I've done everything everyone's asked me to do. Crutches for five weeks. Ice, ice, ice. Working the leg machines. Sitting or standing here like a ghost so I know all the new plays. Working in school—and after school—so I can pass Ms. Rait's class, just so I can play. And now I've got clearance from the doctor—"

"Not yet, you don't have it."

"Well, I *will* have it. And you're saying 'wait till next year'?" Danny paused for a moment, staring at his coach, wanting to say something he couldn't have dreamed of saying until today, and still not sure if he could say it.

"Coach." Danny lowered his voice and took a deep breath. "What happened to my dad taught me that you don't know what next year is gonna be. I might not be here. You might not. We don't know. We know about now, though. We know I'm gonna be back and ready to go, and I still think I'm the guy who's gonna help you win that championship. I just need a chance."

Coach Kinen held his chin. "Well, I'm not saying yes, but I'm not saying no either. We'll see what Doc Severs says on Friday; then I'll make a decision."

Without giving Danny a chance to respond, Coach Kinen blasted his whistle and shouted, "Okay! Line with Coach Willard for one-on-ones! Backs with me for seven-on-seven!"

Off he went, leaving Danny to chew his lip.

56

"You look pretty morose." Ms. Rait sat at her kitchen table with her hands folded.

Danny wrinkled his mouth. "What's that even mean?"

"Glum. Upset. Sad. A good vocabulary word for you." She wrote it out on the scrap paper in front of her. "You can use it on your friends."

"Perfect," he said, slouching down into the chair opposite her. "Where's Mrs. McGillicuddy?"

Ms. Rait took a sip from her glass of iced tea. The cubes clinked. Her face glowed. "I think she had her kittens!"

"What? Really?" Danny stood up and went to the window to look out at the old chicken coop.

"I think so. The door is painted shut, so I can't get in there, but she's in there most of the time, looking slimmer, and acting funny, so . . ."

"How will you get them out?"

"They'll come out when they're ready. I imagine it'll be a couple weeks before you can take one home."

Danny returned to the table and sat down. He hadn't gotten an answer from his mom yet. He planned to just show up with a kitten and hope her heart melted. "Ready?"

"Always." She took out her first sheet and they began to go over it.

They worked hard for an hour. Danny felt good. He was getting it, and Ms. Rait praised him.

"Let's do the practice test," Danny said.

"Um . . . you might want to wait until the weekend. We've got more to do." Ms. Rait tapped her pen on the side of her glass.

"I can do it. C'mon, Ms. Rait. You always say, 'reach for the stars,' so I'm reaching."

She paused and looked at him for a moment. Then she nodded. "Oh, okay. But call your mom and tell her we'll be an hour late. I don't want her to worry."

Danny called his mom, who said it was fine.

Danny took the test. It was harder than he thought. There were words he didn't know and couldn't guess. They left gaping holes in the paragraphs he had to answer questions about. Still, he told himself he only needed two out of every three to be correct, and some answers were easy. He kept his spirits up and handed it over when she said, "Time."

He watched her grade it, slashing the wrong answers with her red marker that left a little streak like blood. Finally, she wrote "57%," circled that in blood, and looked up at him.

"So, I'll pass the real test though, right?" He was smiling, but when he saw the doubt on her face, it melted. "Why are you looking at me like that?"

"Danny, you're doing very well, especially this past week."

"But?"

"But it's a lot to expect that you'll just learn to read fluently and put it all together for the first-marking-period test."

"I'm doing good, so . . . I don't get it. If I'm close, you'll pass me, right?"

She looked at her red marker, then pointed it at herself before pointing it at him. "I won't pass you or fail you, Danny. *You'll* do that. You might pass, but you might not. We've been through this."

Danny pushed his chair back and rose to his feet. "Yeah, but that was a month ago. I've been here every day you asked me. I've done all the work. I read books. And now you're saying you'd fail me? What's wrong with you? I thought we were friends."

"Danny, I'm your teacher. I like you and I care about you. That's why it has to be *you* who does this. No more exceptions."

"That stinks! You're . . . you're just like Coach Kinen." Danny gathered his things. "I do everything you say and you still stab me in the back!"

"I am not Coach Kinen," she said, sputtering.

"No. You're *not*. At least he said he'd think about it before he sticks it to me. I've got a chance with him. But not you. You're the reading police. I gave you everything I have, now just line me up and shoot me. Can I have a blindfold? Will you give me *that*?" Danny grabbed his backpack and raced out of the house.

He was nearly to the center of town when Ms. Rait pulled up beside him in her car and rolled down the window. "Please get in, Danny. I told your mom I'd drive you home."

Danny burned inside with the desire not to get into her car. He did not want to give her anything, but he knew better than to overdo it on his foot this last week. He got in, determined not to say a word.

"Thank you," she said, and began to drive.

Danny didn't have to worry about talking because Ms. Rait wasn't either, until she pulled into his driveway. "I'll be ready for you from six to seven tomorrow. If you come, fine. If not, that's your call. The final is in two weeks, so you're running out of time."

He got out and shut the door.

57

Danny went to Ms. Rait's house after practice the next day. He wasn't going to let her say he didn't do his part. If she failed him, it wasn't going to be because he quit. He knew that's what his dad would have told him, so he did as she asked, but he made no small talk. He didn't ask about her cat or the kittens.

Wednesday night, he woke up screaming. He'd dreamed about the last run with his dad, only in the dream his dad lay there begging Danny for help. Danny stood there, willing his legs to run with every fiber he had, but he couldn't force them to move.

Danny's mom rushed into the room and held him until he stopped screaming and just cried. She told him it was okay, and even heavy with sadness, he remembered Mr. Crenshaw's words and knew that it was okay.

Thursday's game was slow torture. He rode with the team

on the bus to Millerton, his mind blank while everyone around him wound themselves into a frenzy. He sat on the bench, still elevating his foot, but he couldn't avoid seeing Markle go on a romp through the Millerton defense. At one point, Bug appeared and asked Danny to hand him the water bottle resting beside him.

Bug didn't mean anything by it, he was just Bug, but it made Danny feel like a water boy. The ride home was worse. The team chanted Markle's name as he led the cheer like a band director, standing in the middle of the bus. Even Cupcake joined in until he saw Danny glaring at him.

Cupcake shrugged and silently mouthed, "Sorry."

Danny stayed quiet as Herman drove him and Cupcake into town. When they pulled into Rait's driveway, Cupcake spun around from the front seat to address Danny. "Hey, bro. It's all gonna be beef. You'll come back next week and light the world on fire. You'll pass your test and play in the big game. This is all gonna seem like some bad barley dream that's over."

Danny's hand stopped on the door handle and he paused a beat before he looked Cupcake in the eye. "I seriously doubt any of that will happen."

Danny enjoyed the shock on his best friend's face. "Even if the doctor clears me and even if Coach Kinen gives me a chance to win my job back, I'm on track to fail Rait's test and I'll be ineligible for the big game anyway."

"Bro, you've been here every *day*. You're barely on Xbox anymore. You know she's gonna pass you." Cupcake smiled like it was a joke between them.

"No. She's not." Danny didn't wait to continue the

discussion. He got out, thanked Herman, and marched into Rait's house as he heard them pull away.

The next day his mom picked him up after school and took him to the doctor's. They were shown directly into a waiting room without an MRI this time.

"Please take off your shoe and sock," said the nurse who showed them in.

Danny did as he was told. He wiggled his toes and forced a smile at his mom.

Dr. Severs came in after about a half hour.

"So, how's it feeling?" The doctor picked up Danny's foot and immediately put strong pressure on the injured bone.

The way his life was going, Danny was ready for pain, but it didn't come. "Fine."

The doctor held the foot, squeezing harder and searching Danny's face. Danny thought of his dad and his old-school toughness. He'd made it another way. Maybe listening to the doctor's advice—no matter how hard it had been—was new-school toughness. He smiled until the doctor let go.

"Well, it looks good to me." Dr. Severs typed some notes on his laptop. "Keep an eye on it, though. Any pain or swelling and I want to know about it. Got it?"

"Yes, sir." Danny pulled on his sock. He couldn't stop grinning. "Uh, Doctor, could you call Coach Kinen for me and tell him I'm good to go?"

"I'll send him an email." The doctor looked down at his computer and began to type again. "And good luck, Danny.

I'm taking my two boys to the championship. I'm assuming you'll be there. We'll be rooting for you."

The doctor looked up and smiled.

Danny couldn't bring himself to say that he had no idea if he'd even play.

58

Saturday's football practices were when the coaches installed the game plan for their upcoming opponents. Danny got there early and found Coach Kinen in his office making his final notes on the five-by-seven cards where he drew the plays. He put the marker down and pointed to the chair beside his desk.

"Have a seat, Danny."

Danny didn't like the look on his coach's face. He could feel the bad news.

"Coach, I—"

Coach Kinen held up his hand. "Danny, I've given this a lot of thought. I can't make a decision until I see how you look. Maybe you're going to be right where you left off. I don't think so. It's almost impossible for a running back to take six weeks off and just hit the ground running."

Danny wanted to remind Coach Kinen that he wasn't just

any runner. He was Danny Owens, the guy everyone wor-
shipped after the opening game, but he saw that his coach
didn't intend to listen.

"So we'll see how you look running around out there today,
and if you look good, when I get the chance, I'll try and get you
a few live reps with the second team."

"Second?" Danny knew that reps with the second team
meant a line that wasn't as good and a backup quarterback who
was a far cry from Jace, who ran the offense like a Swiss watch.
It would mean quick closing holes, if he had any opening at
all, and a quarterback whose timing and handoffs were rarely
smooth.

Coach Kinen gave him a look of surprise. "You didn't
expect to take reps from Markle, did you? You saw the game
Thursday. You were there. He's been pretty amazing."

Danny wanted to remind his coach that he'd been amazing
too, and that, yes, he did want some of Markle's reps. How
could he compete running only with the second team? But
he said nothing. The look on Coach Kinen's face told him he
couldn't.

"Okay, Coach."

"I'm surprised by your reaction, Danny." The coach
frowned. "I thought you'd be excited for the chance."

Danny swallowed and responded right away. "Yes, sir. I am.
Thank you, sir."

Coach Kinen smiled and leaned back so that his chair
squeaked. "Well, that's okay. You're a good kid and I know next
year you're gonna do great things for us."

Danny's insides chilled. Coach Kinen didn't *want* him to

have a spectacular performance in the big game. He didn't want Danny to be selected for the varsity like his father before him had been. He wanted a star running back on his team next year. Danny stood up with his limbs trembling and left the coach's office.

He dressed in silence and walked out to the field before most guys even arrived at the locker room. He got down in a two-point stance with a football and started to blast his way through the gauntlet machine. But after six weeks away, his timing was off. The arms in the cage battered his upper and lower body, causing unexpected pain. Confused, Danny tumbled down inside the machine, cursing aloud. Panic filled him and he looked toward the locker room to make sure no one had come out early enough to see him. They hadn't, and he struggled to his feet. He had to worm his way out of the gauntlet because the only way to get through it clean was to hit it running and not stop.

He'd just freed himself from the machine when he saw Jace and Duval Carmody exit the locker room and head toward the field. Instead of trying again, he ran through the ropes, lifting his knees high. It hurt, but it didn't trip him up. He should have done it first. It got his legs moving and warm.

"Hey, Danny," Jace called, "come catch with us."

"Sure." Danny swelled with pride to have Jace treat him this way, and he hustled over to work with them while Jace loosened his arm.

"So you're back." Jace gunned a pass at Duval, who snatched it from the air before tucking it under his arm briefly and then passing it back to Danny.

Danny caught the ball and handed it to Jace. "Yeah. Not with the first team, though."

"Really?" Jace stopped and looked at him before passing it to Duval again. "Well, Markle has looked pretty good. I still think you're better."

"Thanks, Jace. I wish you were the coach."

"I'll talk to him."

Danny caught Duval's pass. "To Coach Kinen?"

"He listens to me sometimes." Jace accepted the ball, spun it to find the laces, and rifled it to Duval.

Danny didn't know, but certainly there was a chance that Jace could make a difference.

Practice began and Danny gave everything he had. He was in high gear when he went through agilities, running like his life depended on it while the others moaned and groaned, still sore from Thursday's game. Danny didn't care about the dirty looks from his teammates that told him to back down because he was making everyone look like loafers. That's what he wanted.

When Coach Kinen led them to the gauntlet, Danny jumped to the front of the line. He stared at the stiff arms, waiting to make him look like a fool, and took a deep breath. He wondered if jumping to the front had been a mistake, but before he could have another thought, Coach Kinen blew his whistle.

Jace said, "Set, hut!"

Danny leapt forward, took the handoff from Jace, and hit the machine. He burst through the arms with his legs pumping like the pistons of a race car. He came out the other side, circled the manacle, and tossed the ball to his coach like it was no big deal, even though it was.

As practice went on, he felt himself getting better and more confident. He felt certain Coach Kinen saw how well he was doing. You'd have to be blind not to, and it made Danny oh-so-hungry to get that ball in his hands during a live drill.

After a water break, Coach yelled for an inside run. Danny got giddy. It would be his first shot to really show what he could do. He raced over to the drill, arriving first in case Coach decided to reward him for his great effort so far.

He didn't.

Coach called for the first offense, and they began a steady pounding of the mostly second-team defense. Danny shifted from foot to foot, stretching his legs to keep them fresh and wondering if Jace had forgotten what he'd said before practice.

After Markle's seventh carry in eight plays, Jace jogged over to Coach Kinen and had some private words.

Danny's muscles tightened.

Danny watched Coach Kinen's face change colors as it twisted into a snarl.

"What do you think? This is a *democracy*!?"

Jace's face fell. He wagged his head. "No, Coach."

"So get out of my face!" Coach Kinen swung his arm up, pointing for Jace to go. "Maybe we should take a vote on quarterback! Maybe Bug should be our Q-One! I know his momma'd be happy!"

Coach Kinen's eyes darted toward Danny next, and Danny felt the sting before he cast his eyes to the ground.

He didn't get a single rep with the first team. He didn't get one with the second team, either. And, as practice ended with cross-field sprints, the ache in Danny's heart had him lagging behind.

Not that anyone cared.

"So, how was your weekend?" Mr. Crenshaw looked up from his desk, where he was reading a book that Danny sounded out as *Master and Commander*.

Danny sat down on the couch and took out the Playaway as well as a paperback copy of *Maniac Magee*. Then he got right to it. "Do you believe in heaven and the other place?"

Mr. Crenshaw put his book down. "You went to church? Nice."

"No. My weekend was the other place."

"So, bad?"

"Maybe worse," Danny said. "And *she* didn't help matters."

"'She' is either your mom, Janey Kurtz, or Ms. Rait."

"Your girlfriend, and her test."

Mr. Crenshaw looked at him blankly.

Danny huffed. That was Mr. Crenshaw's go-to whenever

Ms. Rait came up—a blank face. "Ms. Rait."

Danny told him the story of yet another practice test he'd failed, how he'd studied English instead of going to the bonfire, and the disaster of Saturday's practice.

"That's tough. Coach Kinen's a tough customer." Mr. Crenshaw moved to the chair facing the couch across the low table where the checkerboard now lay.

"You know him?" Danny asked.

"Faculty meetings. Also, when you were sent to see me, he worked me over pretty good about helping you, so I know he's on your side."

"*Was* on my side," Danny said. "Everyone was until I got hurt. Now, it's like I'm nothing."

"Your real friends don't think that." Mr. C moved a checker to kick off a game. "I don't think that."

Danny looked at the piece and shook his head. "No, thanks. I'm tired of games."

Mr. Crenshaw raised an eyebrow. "Some people say life's a game."

"Well, there you go. I'm sick of that game too. I'm sick of losing."

Mr. Crenshaw sat back in his chair. "Come on, Danny. That's not like you, talking about losing, down on yourself. Life is full of challenges and obstacles. It's about how we respond when we get knocked down. If someone tackled you on the field, I can't believe you'd stop playing. You'd get up, take that guy's number, and run over him the next time, right?"

Danny frowned. "I can't get on the field. That's the problem. I'm not gonna get the chance to knock anyone down unless I push someone and they trip over the bench."

"Things change, Danny. We never know what tomorrow holds." Mr. C pointed at the book beside Danny on the couch. "I bet you didn't think you'd be able to read just a few weeks ago."

Danny looked down at the book and snorted. "When I saw the cover I sounded it out as 'man-i-ack.' I had no idea what a man-i-ack was. Then I turned on the Playaway and ta-da! It's 'mane-ee-ack.' How does an 'i' make an 'ee' sound? The only thing that's a bigger mess than my life is the English language."

62

It was a rough week for Danny. He felt like he was spinning his wheels with the whole reading project. The new material was really difficult, and he seemed to be going backward on the material he'd already learned and thought he knew. Ms. Rait was down on him and warned him several times that he wouldn't pass unless he made more progress. And at football practice, things actually got worse. He'd stopped trying as hard at the individual drills because Coach Kinen wouldn't even look at him, let alone put him in for some live action.

Then Thursday happened.

Danny stood in the pouring rain. Drops of water rolled down his helmet, spattering off the rubber-coated metal facemask and wetting his face with a fine mist. He and the rest of the scrubs were huddled together on the sideline, like Cupcake's cows on a frosty winter's night.

This game at Layton Forks was supposed to be in the bag. The team was the doormat of Jericho County football and the only thing between Crooked Creek and the big game. It was late in the third quarter, and if Danny were to be totally honest, he'd have to admit that he didn't care that the scoreboard read HOME 13, VISITORS 0 through the misty wet. Thinking back to the week of practice, he'd heard Coach Kinen scolding the team for goofing off and not taking Layton Forks seriously, which they hadn't.

At the time, Danny couldn't have cared less. He'd been too

busy licking his own wounds. And now, it was nearly enjoyable to watch Coach Kinen's purple-faced tirade at Markle for fumbling the ball no less than three times in the wet, muddy slop. After Markle's fourth fumble, Danny crossed his arms and moved closer to the show. A small spark in his mind hinted at a change in the running back position.

Markle sulked off the field, kicking mud like a spoiled three-year-old. Coach Kinen met him at the edge of the field. The coach said something and when Markle shrugged, Coach Kinen went berserk. "Take a seat, Markle! You're *done!*"

A jolt of excitement straightened Danny's spine. The wet discomfort slipped away. Coach Kinen turned and surveyed the sideline.

When his eyes met Danny's, everything about Danny's appearance said he was ready to go.

Coach Kinen seemed to be considering Danny. Maybe he was recalling all that hard work he'd done before he gave up trying to impress anyone. Or, maybe he was remembering that Danny had, in fact, given up. Danny tried to look confident, but he felt like a pathetic puppy, begging for a table scrap he'd never get.

When Coach Kinen's eyes kept going, Danny's shoulders slumped.

"Scott Port!" Coach Kinen shouted so everyone could hear. "You take running back on the next series! Let's see if we can get someone who can hang on to the ball!"

Danny stood for a while by himself, not to be too obvious about wanting to get in the game. He felt a nudge and turned to find Cupcake, lathered with sweat despite the rain.

"Bro, he shoulda put you in." Cupcake spoke under his

breath as he fished a slab of mud wedged between his facemask and helmet. "I thought he was gonna for sure. Scott's a speedster. He can't run in this mess."

"Doesn't matter." Danny shrugged and pretended to be interested in their defense. "I'm probably gonna fail Rait's test anyway, so it just saves me from being ineligible for the big game and losing my mind."

Cupcake peered at him through the raindrops like his body had been taken over by aliens. "Yeah. I guess that's true."

Cupcake walked away and Danny watched the Layton Forks offense sputter and have to punt. Jake Moreland signaled fair catch and muffed it, but somehow he got the ball back from under the pile of bodies. Scott Port glowed in his bright white uniform among all the mud-covered players in the huddle. He was like a beacon for the defense to zero in on, and that's what they did.

Scott's first carry went for negative three yards. His next carry he tried to cut too fast, slipped, and lost two yards. On third down, he slipped again, then fumbled a toss sweep, giving up the ball to Layton Forks on the seventeen-yard line going in. Scott jogged off the field with his head hanging. He made a beeline to Coach Kinen to take his verbal punishment like a man, but their coach ignored Scott and instead focused on the defense.

Layton Forks scored two plays later.

Danny thought it served Coach Kinen right, turning to Scott, a speed back, when Danny could have replaced Markle and given the team new life—which it desperately needed if they were going to pull out a win and head to the championship.

But that's not what happened, and now, given the bad weather and Layton Forks' three-touchdown lead, you could almost stick a fork in this game because it was practically done.

Danny turned away and listened to the patter of rain against the shell of his helmet. He was aware of the ball being kicked off out on the field, and some shouting on his sideline, but he ignored the game because it had nothing to do with him.

That's when Cupcake grabbed him by the arm and swung him around. "Bro, what are you doing? Coach is calling for you."

Danny yanked free. "Not funny, Cupcake."

"Bro—"

"Owens! Are you deaf! Get over here!"

Danny spun around and saw his coach scowling. Water dripped from the bill of his cap.

Danny bolted toward the coach, stopping in front of him in a state of total confusion. "Yes, sir?"

Coach Kinen looked him up and down like a used car before he huffed and then spoke. "You can't be worse than what we've had already. Can you get me some yards if I put you in?"

Danny spoke without thinking. "Yes, sir."

"Go on then." Coach Kinen waved him onto the field.

Danny snapped his chinstrap as he jogged out toward the huddle. His legs were stiff from just standing in the rain, and he wondered how wise he'd been to jump into the fray without warming up. He joined the circle around Jace.

The quarterback blew some water off his lips and peered up at Danny. "Give us something, Danny. Trips right twenty-eight power sweep on two. Ready . . . break!"

Danny lined up and looked over the defense. Linebackers with mud-smeared faces snarled at him through the rain. Jace had begun his cadence. Danny reminded himself of the play as the ball was snapped. He took off to the right side, slipped, and regained his footing in time to see the pitch sail past him and skid to a spinning stop in the mud.

The defense shouted, "Fumble!"

Danny tried to redirect and slipped again. An outside line-backer shot past him, belly-flopping on the ball. The impact spit the ball sideways toward Danny. He scooped it up and began to run the opposite way.

As soon as he turned, he got a mouthful of a Layton Forks shoulder pad. He saw stars and his back struck the ground with a thud. He lay there clutching the ball, breathless in the mud, blinking up into the rainy gray mist.

"You get up. You get up, Danny," his father said sternly. "I don't care if you never even make it to the varsity, but you get up when you get knocked down."

Danny was halfway to his feet without thinking, and he looked around. He'd heard his father's voice. It frightened him, but it also warmed his heart.

"You gotta run north and south in the mud. Never run for the sideline. You run straight up with your head high and you keep your feet under you. Keep them pumping. I know, that's not how you're supposed to run—unless you're in the mud. If it's ever a mess like today, you keep your feet and you'll tear it up while everyone else is slip-sliding away."

Danny looked around him to see if anyone else had heard his father's speech, the same one he'd given Danny the morn-ing of his first Pop Warner game in the mud. All he saw was Cupcake. "You okay, Danny?"

"I don't know," he said.

"Danny!" Coach Kinen was screaming from the sideline.

"Get your head out of your butt or I'll yank you too!"

Danny nodded that he'd heard and got into the huddle.

Jace's look accused Danny of negligence on the last play.

"I slipped." It was all Danny could say.

"Okay," Jace said, "trips left twenty-seven power sweep on one, re—"

"Wait!" Danny shouted, holding out both hands to stop Jace from breaking the huddle. "Don't run that. Run twenty-one counter trap."

Jace removed his mouthpiece so he could be heard more clearly. "Danny, I don't call the plays, Coach Kinen does, and he called twenty-seven sweep."

"I'm telling you, just listen . . . it's too sloppy. We can't run to the outside, but I can take it up the middle. You gotta run north and south in the mud. Please, Jace, give me a chance. I know I can do this, but a sweep won't work."

"I'm not changing the play. I can't," Jace said.

"Okay, but I can. I'll take total responsibility. This is all on me. You guys are witnesses. I told you I won't run anything but the trap."

Jace looked around the huddle.

Bug said, "Do it."

Carmody said, "Go for it."

Cupcake said, "Why not?"

Jace huffed and shook his head in doubt. "Well, if something doesn't work, this is my last rodeo with Coach Kinen anyway.

"Okay, trips left twenty-one counter trap on one, ready . . . break!"

Danny lined up behind his quarterback. He wiggled his feet into the mud for a hold. Jace called the cadence and took the snap. Danny began pumping his legs as he moved forward.

He ran straight up and down, his legs pumping like pistons.

The defensive tackle came right at Danny, unblocked. It was the kind of collision every defender dreams of, but at the last instant before they hit, Cupcake flashed across Danny's vision, crushing the unsuspecting defender with a trap block. Danny kept going, his legs pumping like a boxer's hands working a speed bag.

He shot through the line and met a linebacker who banged into Danny before slipping off. Danny did a dance spin and kept going. The safety grabbed him from behind, then jumped on his back. Danny remembered chicken fights on the playground and kept going. Another linebacker caught up and wrapped his arms around Danny's waist.

He kept going.

It took two more players to finally drag him down after a twenty-three-yard gain and a first down. Cupcake arrived and began shoving defenders off of Danny before helping him to his feet and banging facemasks with a hug.

"Yeah, bro! That's grade-A beef!"

Danny let Cupcake escort him to the huddle as he looked to the sideline for Coach Kinen's reaction.

"Yes!" Coach Kinen ran up the sideline, pumping his fist. He apparently didn't even realize they'd changed the play.

Danny's other teammates tried to shower him with back slaps but Cupcake fended them off. "My bro needs some air. Chill, guys. Chill. He's gonna do it again."

He did do it, all the way to the end zone.

Crooked Creek came alive, on the field and in the stands. After Danny's touchdown, the defense swarmed the field and shut down their opponents the way they'd expected to all week. Duval Carmody blocked a punt and Crooked Creek took over on the thirty-six-yard line going in. It took Danny and the offense just four plays to reach the end zone. After another successful extra point, they were only down by six with the scoreboard now reading 20–14.

The clock read 4:27, so they had time, but not much. After a deep kickoff that pinned Layton Forks down on their twenty-three, the defense roared out onto the gridiron. Danny stood on the sideline with his teammates, shouting encouragement. They stopped the first two plays at the line and the sideline began to celebrate, the offensive players eager to get the ball back.

On third-and-ten, Layton Forks' quarterback rolled right and threw a wobbling duck of a pass ten yards outside his open wide receiver. Danny and his teammates were already airborne, jumping for joy when Markle appeared from nowhere and hammered the defenseless receiver, knocking him to the muck.

Flags and whistles came from every direction.

"Markle!" Coach Kinen yanked off his hat and stomped it into the mud. "What's *wrong* with you?! Are you *kidding* me? Out! *Get out! You're done!*"

Markle skulked off the field and pushed his way through the team to the bench, where he slammed his helmet down. Danny would have been delighted at Markle's complete undoing had it not put them into such a terrible position and seriously jeopardized their amazing comeback. Markle's fifteen-yard unsportsmanlike penalty advanced Layton Forks to the thirty-eight and gave them a fresh set of downs.

The clock now read 3:08, and unless Coach Kinen used their valuable time-outs, Layton Forks could run the clock down to a minute and change, punt the ball, and force Danny's team to pass the ball in the rain. Running the ball sixty or seventy yards would be nearly impossible with that little amount of time since the clock continued on a run play unless the ball went out-of-bounds. Danny couldn't help suspecting that Markle knew what he was doing when he laid out the receiver after the whistle.

Coach Kinen chose to burn his time-outs to stop the clock. Their defense held. Layton Forks punted, and Danny's team got the ball back on the thirty-nine-yard line. They had to go sixty-one yards in less than three minutes.

Coach Kinen grabbed Danny by the facemask and pulled him close before he ran out to the huddle. "You gotta get to the sideline and get out-of-bounds. We can run it, but you have to stop the clock. Got it?"

"*North and south!*"

"Coach?" Danny's eyes widened. "Did you say 'north and south'?"

Coach Kinen gave Danny's helmet a little shake. "No! I said, *Get to the sideline.*"

Danny was confused. "But . . . you gotta run north and south in the mud."

Coach Kinen stared hard into Danny's eyes. "Danny, are you okay?"

Coach Kinen gently smacked the side of Danny's helmet. "Danny? I said, 'Are you okay?'"

"Yeah, Coach."

"Let's go, Coach!" one of the refs shouted.

"Okay. Go." Coach shoved Danny toward the huddle.

When he got there, he asked Jace the play.

"Twenty-eight sweep."

"No. Don't do it. Go twenty-four dive."

"Danny, Coach said get out-of-bounds. You gotta run to the sideline."

Danny stared wildly around the huddle. "Guys, you gotta remember these plays: twenty-four dive, twenty-three dive, twenty-two trap, twenty-one trap, and twenty draw. It's easy: twenty-four, twenty-three, twenty-two, twenty-one, twenty. We can't huddle, and we have to get right up to the line."

"What if we need more plays?" Jace asked. "The clock will be running."

"Everything is on one. If we get past twenty, we run a freeze play and draw them offside. That'll stop the clock and we can huddle and call more plays."

"What if the freeze doesn't work?" Jace's voice broke.

"It will." Danny looked around. "Come on, guys. We got this. Twenty-four, three, two, one, zero. Next stop is the big game. Ready . . . break!"

Danny gained just six on the first play. He could hear Coach Kinen howling from the sideline. "What are you *doing*!?"

Danny ignored him. He lined up and broke the twenty-four dive for fifteen. Thirty yards to go, and the clock ticking down at 1:57.

This time, as they lined up, Danny saw the defense collapsing into the middle. They had a wedge of players there to make an inside run nearly impossible.

Jace got behind the center and shouted, "Hot! Hot! Hot!"

Jace tapped his helmet and looked out at Moreland, who also tapped his helmet. Jace called the cadence and took the snap. Jace flipped his hips and fired a hitch pass to Moreland. The ball slipped and wobbled and flew up into the air. Moreland raced toward it, scooped it just before it hit the ground, and kept going. A Forks linebacker popped Moreland dead-on, bouncing him back the way he'd come.

Moreland caught his balance, turned, and raced for the sideline. He gained eight yards and stopped the clock. With the ball on the twenty-two, the clock froze at 1:39.

Coach Kinen was a madman on the sideline, but he had

no time-outs and Jace was ignoring him. They had time for a huddle now, and Jace addressed Danny.

"They loaded the box, so I figured I better throw it once to spread them out."

"Great idea," Danny said, then he nodded at Moreland. "Awesome play, Jake."

"Let's keep going with your plays." Jace looked around the huddle. "Twenty-two, then twenty-one and twenty. Freeze if we need it. Everything's on one. Ready . . . break!"

The twenty-two went for just five yards, but the twenty-one gave them ten. On the seven-yard line, Bug slipped and let his man right through on the twenty draw. The defender slipped, too, and submarined Danny's ankles just as he took the hand-off. Danny took a spill for a three-yard loss. The clock was down to just eighteen seconds.

Everyone scrambled to the line as the clock ticked.

The freeze play was just what it said. After going on the first "hut" five times in a row, the defense typically got lulled into a rhythm and would jump forward on the quarterback's first "hut" the sixth time. The resulting offside penalty would give the offense five more yards toward the end zone and, mercifully, stop the play clock so time wouldn't run out on Crooked Creek and end the game.

At nine seconds on the clock, Danny knew that it was all or nothing, so he froze. Jace began his cadence. "Down! Blue ten! Blue ten! Set . . ."

68

"HUT!"

The same lineman who'd tackled Danny in the backfield jumped the gun. Flags flew. Whistles shrieked. The D lineman slapped his own helmet.

Danny's team pumped their fists and slapped high fives. The refs marched off the penalty and put the ball down on the five-yard line. The clock had stopped at five seconds. They had one play and Coach Kinen was going bananas on the sideline, signaling his choice.

"What's he want?" Danny asked in the huddle.

"Danny, if we win and I don't call his play, I'm not sure it'll even be worth it," Jace said.

"What play?"

"Twenty-six veer. It's not north and south."

Danny bit his mouthpiece hard. "It's north by northwest . . . Let's do it."

"Yes!"

His offensive teammates all agreed.

It would have been a great story to tell his grandkids if he'd plowed over five defenders and battled his way over the line through a pile of bodies.

But that wasn't what happened.

69

Cupcake and Bug plowed open a hole the size of a bowling alley.

Danny chugged in and scored.

Whistles blew.

The game ended, and the celebration began.

"The veer! The veer! The veer!" Coach Kinen was out on the field hugging Danny and Jace. "It was wide open! I knew it!"

The coach pulled their heads even closer to his. "I don't know what the heck you two were thinking calling all those plays . . .

"But *I love it*!"

They all laughed and suddenly the wet didn't seem so wet and the sky didn't seem so gray. They accepted the thin cheers from the faithful few who'd made the trip in the rain, mostly parents like Danny's mom who'd come despite him telling her not to. They burst out in a soggy, muted applause beneath their umbrellas as the team marched past the stands, heading for the bus.

Danny found his mom and grinned at her, waving a half-raised hand so his teammates wouldn't call him a mama's boy. On board the bus, guys shed their shoulder pads, steaming up the windows. Once they'd all found a seat, Coach Kinen stood up to address them.

"Guys," he said, his voice raspy from yelling in the damp, "I want you all to enjoy this win."

Cheers erupted.

Coach held up his hands for silence and got it. "It wasn't what we thought it was gonna be, but I told you all week that you were takin' this team too light, and what happened?"

"Danny happened!" someone shouted.

Everyone laughed.

Coach Kinen smiled and held up his hands. He nodded. "Yeah, Danny happened. Yes, he did. And that's a lesson, too. Because you never know, in football or in life, when your turn is gonna come. And when it does? Well, I'm bettin' Danny'll tell you, you gotta be ready for it. And if you are? Well, that's how you win championships, and that's what we all . . . are about to do in *the big game*!"

More cheers, and Coach sat down. The driver put the bus in gear and they sang all the way home.

Danny felt the difference on the bus ride to school on Friday. People were doing that thing again where he'd glance their way and they'd pretend they hadn't been looking at him. It made him smile, and he put an arm around Janey's shoulders as they walked into the building, hugging her close.

"Wow. Is it my birthday?" Janey's laughter bubbled up into the cool morning air left behind by the rain.

"Just happy is all." He gave her one more squeeze and then let go. "Back to the land of the living."

"I'm so happy for you."

"You keep saying that."

She shrugged. "I keep feeling it. Now you've got all the motivation you need to study this weekend. I've got it all scheduled out. I've got soccer practice Saturday early in the afternoon, and you have football practice in the morning, but we can work after that. And Sunday, other than church, I'm all yours. I think you should get in one last session with Ms. Rait. Maybe she could meet with you early Saturday afternoon, or Sunday morning. She doesn't seem the church type."

They reached his locker first and he spun the dial. "No, she doesn't. She's the devil."

"Stop it." She lightly slapped his arm. "That's not what I meant and I think you know it."

"The guys on the team think she is, I can tell you that." Danny shoved his backpack into the locker and removed some books and folders with his Playaway. "They're talking about running her out of town this weekend so she can't even give her test on Monday."

"What's that mean, Danny?" Janey looked concerned.

"I don't know." Danny slammed his locker shut, unconcerned. "Scare her or something. Probably some crank phone calls. Heavy breathing. Soap her windows. Stupid stuff, I bet. I'm planning to take the test, if that's what you're worried about."

Janey headed toward her locker now. "I'm worried about her."

"Trust me, she can take care of herself," Danny said.

Janey stopped and looked up at him. "You're not going to do anything to her, though. Right?"

"No," Danny scoffed.

As much as he hated Ms. Rait's rigid rules, he could never bring himself to do something that would scare her. As she spun the dial on her locker, he said, "The guys want to win this championship, though. It's a big deal, and they know they need me. Dillon's defense has six shutouts and they've only given up twenty-six points all season."

"Maybe you should tell Mr. Crenshaw," Janey said, clanking open the locker. "Just so she's ready."

Danny took her by the arm. "Janey, you can't say anything about this to anyone. The guys would kill me. Most of the team doesn't even know. It's just some eighth graders who told me in the locker room last night not to worry, that they'd take care of it."

Janey frowned. "That doesn't sound good to me. And you know about it, so if something bad happens, you're gonna be part of it."

"Shh!" Danny looked around and put his mouth near her ear, whispering. "I am not part of anything. I don't even know what 'it' is. You gotta promise me, Janey, promise me you won't say a word to anyone."

He stepped back and looked into her face. Her eyes swam with worry and doubt.

Finally, she gave a short nod. "Okay."

"Okay. Good." The first bell rang and he turned to go. "See you in Rait's."

"See you."

71

"I heard my dad talking to me." Danny hadn't intended to tell anyone, but the words spilled from his mouth after just five minutes of chess. Mr. Crenshaw was teaching him to play.

Mr. C paused. He held a bishop above the board. He looked at Danny, then took his pawn. "Like, you remembered something he said?"

Danny used a knight to take the bishop. "No. I heard him. His voice. He told me you have to run north and south in the mud."

Mr. Crenshaw nodded at the board. "Good move. What's that mean? North? Mud?"

Danny explained what it all meant and then told Mr. C about hearing his dad twice, and about the impact it had on him and his team.

"You told your teammates?"

"No, but I was so amped up, they listened to me."

Mr. C sat back in his chair. "Well, the human mind is a mystery. How did you feel? When you heard him?"

Danny looked at the wall. "I don't know. . . . Excited? Scared? It made me take over the huddle. I mean, I'd never have done what I did unless it was my *actual dad* telling me. You don't just change the play your coach calls."

"How do you feel now? About your dad?" Mr. C asked.

Danny paused. A wave of emotion began to rock his insides. He bit his cheek to hold back some tears. "Sad. I miss him. . . ."

"I'm sorry," Mr. Crenshaw whispered. "I really am."

"Yeah, well." Danny sniffed and wiped his eyes with the palm of his hand.

"You're doing really well, Danny."

"I am?" He looked at the counselor through a kaleidoscope of tears.

"Yeah. Really well."

"Cuz I'm crying?"

"Cuz you're healing." Mr. C reached down and moved a pawn into position to take Danny's knight.

Danny moved the knight forward with his eyes on a castle. "And?"

"And what?" Mr. C raised an eyebrow.

"You sound like there's an 'and' coming," Danny said.

Mr. C nodded. "And, you don't need to be here every morning. As much as I've enjoyed our time together, there are other kids who need me more than you do."

Danny snorted. "Like Markle."

"Is he having problems?"

"Nothing. Forget it."

"You're upset?" Mr. C asked.

"No. I'm fine." Danny looked down.

"How about Mondays and Fridays?" Mr. Crenshaw said. "We can start and end the week together."

Danny raised his head. "Really? So, we're not just ending?"

Mr. Crenshaw smiled and reached for his queen. He moved it across the entire board. "We can't just end now. I've got to teach you to play chess."

He set the queen down and smiled. "Checkmate."

Practice Friday afternoon and Saturday morning were sweet dreams. Coach Kinen treated Danny like gold.

"What do you think about that play, Danny? You like it?"

"How's your foot doing? Let's not overdo things. We need you for the game."

The downside to all that positive attention was the glaring difference he felt when he walked into Ms. Rait's house Saturday afternoon for what would be the last time. Turned out she *was* a church person, but she said she thought meeting Saturday afternoon was a good idea.

"Danny." She sat at the kitchen table looking like she'd tasted a lemon. She set her book down on the table and began shuffling papers out of her folder, snapping them down in front of him.

"Ma'am." Danny sat.

She dove right in, teaching him some new things and drilling him on the old. She had him answer worksheets on the stopwatch and she brandished her red marker when he'd finished, clicking her tongue and fouling the paper with her red ink.

After a particularly bad page, she pushed it away from her and huffed. "This just isn't good enough. I need more from you. Give me more. The test is Monday."

Danny bit down on the inside of his lip. Obviously, no one from the team had done anything to frighten Ms. Rait or back her down in any way. He kept on, though, because now he really needed this. His dream of the big game had come and gone and come again. He was so close, and instead of moaning to himself, he hunkered down and poured every ounce of energy and concentration he had into learning as much as he possibly could.

He knew the course of his entire life might be changed by a single answer. He needed a 65 percent, that was all.

It wasn't until the sun dipped into the back windows that Ms. Rait rested her red marker on the table between them.

She sat back and sighed heavily.

She looked almost sad.

Danny swallowed, afraid to ask, but knowing he had to.

"So do you think I can do this? You think I can pass?"

73

Ms. Rait picked up her red marker and tapped it against the
table. "When you're about to play one of your football games,
do you ask your coach if he thinks you can win?"

Danny snorted. "No."

"But you're asking me." She puckered her lips and moved
them sideways for a brief moment. "Why would you do that?"

"This is a *test*," Danny said. "Not a game."

Danny couldn't help feeling annoyed. He knew he should
hold his temper, but it burned him to have spent his afternoon
slaving away only to be criticized for asking someone's opinion.
That's all he was doing.

"A test that's more important than a game," she continued.
"A test that could make the game irrelevant."

"You're not my coach," he said.

"You better believe I'm not."

Danny searched her face. Was that a smile lurking there beneath its surface? It made him choke with anger.

He pounded a fist on the table and jumped to his feet. "Fine! You want to play games with me? Go for it! But watch your back, lady! We're tight in this town!"

Danny stormed out of the house, right out the back door. Mrs. McGillicuddy yowled and burst from beneath the steps, startling him so that he ran into her. The cat ran for cover, zipping into the chicken coop like a flash of light.

"Danny! You get back here!" Ms. Rait shouted. Danny could hear her clearly through the open windows, but he kept walking. "You think I'm intimidated? By anyone? You're wrong!"

Danny covered his ears and took off running.

74

Danny ate a silent dinner with his mom. He knew she'd grown used to his bouts of quiet. She'd told him so before. He wondered if she'd spoken to Mr. C about it, and if he'd told her it was normal.

That set him to wondering how Mr. C could ever want to be around someone as rigid and grouchy as Rait.

His mom cleared her throat. "Anything I can help you with?"

He looked up, startled. "No. I'm good. I'll help you clean up. Janey's coming to study, and I think we're going to a bonfire after."

"Bonfire?"

"Just some guys on the team, behind the old concrete factory. It's like a celebration."

She frowned at him. "There's no beer, right?"

"Mom, we're football players. Everyone goes."

Her face softened. "I used to go to bonfires with your father—" She looked at Danny, stricken. "I didn't mean to say that. . . ."

"It's okay, Mom. I miss him too." Danny felt his eyes tear and he looked down and wiped them on his sleeve. "Dad would be so proud to see how you've quit drinking. And made a start on quitting smoking, too."

"Oh, Danny." His mom circled the table, pulled up a chair, and hugged him to her. She was crying softly too, and Danny let his own tears go. The bones in her arms cut into his shoulders and back, but somehow it felt comforting.

They sat that way for several minutes, just breathing, with the late-day sun slanting in through the window, before there was a knock at the back door.

Danny jumped up, wiping frantically at his face. "It's Janey."

He stopped with his hand on the knob and looked back at his mom, who was wiping her own eyes. "Okay?"

She sniffed and nodded and he swung the door open. "Hi."

"Hey." Janey peered past him. "Is everything okay?"

"Yeah." He motioned her in. "Just talking about my dad, so . . ."

"I can come back," Janey said.

"You come right in." Danny's mom hopped up from her chair with a smile. "We're just fine. Aren't we, Danny?"

"Yeah." Danny smiled because it was true. He took a breath. "Nothing wrong with being sad. Come on. We can study in my room."

Danny tried, but whether it was his emotional day or just being burned out from all his mental exercise with Ms. Rait, he just couldn't get his brain engaged. After an hour and a half, he stopped faking it.

"C'mon," he said, pushing back his chair from the desk. "I can't do it anymore. I just can't. Maybe tomorrow, but not now."

Janey looked at him doubtfully. "I'm okay, but are you sure?"

"Yeah." Danny looked at the time. "It's dark out. That bonfire's probably already going. Let's eat something and go hang out, and then I can walk you home."

His mom fed them a pasta casserole. They said goodbye and set out for town, walking along Route 222 with only two vehicles passing by to disrupt their nighttime walk. In town, they took to the sidewalks until they ran out on the far side, and then they walked on the shoulder for the remaining quarter mile to the abandoned concrete factory.

The factory rose up, an inky fortress against the starlit sky. The chain-link gates sagged open. They passed through, and even before they rounded the corner they could see the orange glow and hear the thump and twang of country music from a boom box.

Dark figures milled about around a huge fire with ten-foot tongues of flame licking the night. Danny saw Cupcake's massive shape, and he tapped him on the back.

"Hey!" Cupcake turned Danny's way, then turned back toward the fire. "Hey, everybody! Danny's here!"

A cheer went up.

Danny saw the smiling faces of his teammates as well as the faces of other boys and girls flickering in the orange light. Many of them he recognized from school. Cupcake reached into a cooler and took two cans of Coke from their icy bath, handing them to Danny and Janey.

"Janey!" Cupcake bellowed and gave her a hug.

Danny cracked his can open with a hiss. He swapped it with Janey's and opened that one for himself. He liked the way she went along as if she expected him to open one for her.

Jace appeared, wearing a Crooked Creek Football hoodie. "Dan-eee! This your girlfriend?"

Danny laughed. "No. My friend. This is Janey. Janey, Jace. The quarterback."

"I know," Janey said.

"Well, if she's not your girlfriend, maybe she'll be mine. Kelly and I are on the rocks." Jace laughed.

Danny thought he was more serious than joking, but he relaxed when Janey said, "Thanks, but no thanks."

She looked at Danny with a glowing smile that made his heart gallop.

"Too late, I see," Jace said. "Just like I was too late for the de-Rait."

"De-what?" Danny asked.

Cupcake laughed. "De-Rait, as in Ms. Rait. Bug and some of the guys left about ten minutes ago to hint that she might want to make Crooked Creek part of her past."

Danny chuckled. "Ugh. She was pure evil to me today. What are they doing? Egging her windows?"

Jace laughed. "Naw. You know Bug, *Fire*bug. Evidently she's got some old abandoned chicken coop in her backyard. Man, I guess Bug was like a dog in a butcher shop when he saw that old, broken-down thing. . . . It's the ultimate prank!"

Jace grinned around at them all. The flicker of orange light and black shadows gave him the look of a madman.

Danny's mouth fell open. "What?"

"Yeah," Jace said, still grinning, "they're gonna burn it down."

"No!" Danny screamed, and he took off running.

"Hey!" Jace screamed after him. "There's nothing in it!"

But Danny knew there was.

75

Danny ran right down the middle of the road. He hit the center of town and went left, cutting the corner on the sidewalk past the drugstore and out into the street again under the lights. A pickup truck screeched its brakes and blared its horn, just missing him. Danny never slowed down.

His breath began to flag as he passed the last houses packed into the tight cluster of town. In the back of his mind he knew he had about a half mile to go. His lungs were blazing and he gasped for breath. His stomach heaved, and he left what remained of his dinner on the road without breaking stride.

He thought the next thing would be a total collapse—that his body would just give out beneath him like a spent mule. But this was the kind of pain he could run through. His eyes spilled tears in the wind. He willed himself on, his pace slowing despite his determination. His legs had no feeling, and they began to wobble. He was almost there!

But when he saw the flickering orange glow outlining the roofline of Ms. Rait's house, he knew he was too late.

He kept going anyway, and he was glad he did. Flames engulfed the back of the coop and danced across the slanted roof, leaping for the stars.

"Mrs. McGillicuddy!" Danny screamed at the top of his lungs. "Mrs. McGillicuddy!"

Smoke poured from the entrance like a factory stack until it spit out Mrs. McGillicuddy with a kitten in her mouth.

"Oh, Mrs. McGillicuddy!" Danny sobbed at the sight of her, but the cat paid him no mind. She dropped the kitten beside another in the grass right up next to the house—Danny didn't know if they were even alive—and then, in a streak of white, she raced right back into the burning coop.

The coop stood off the ground on stacks of cinder blocks. On the side was a door and beneath it a jumbled pile of blocks that years ago had served as stairs for the farmer's wife to harvest her eggs. Danny raced up the steps and tried the door. It was jammed shut.

He grabbed the old wooden handle with both hands and pulled for all he was worth. The handle broke and he tumbled backward, but he sprang to his feet like after a tackle. This time he kicked the door. His foot went right through and a plume of smoke rushed out.

The fire was roaring above him, and he could feel the heat. He put both hands into the hole he'd kicked and yanked again. This time the door gave way. A great gust of smoke surrounded him, but it escaped skyward and he could see the puffy white shape of Mrs. McGillicuddy in the far corner of the coop in a nest of rags and dusty hay on the floor.

She was curled up and lay still. He presumed the smoke had done her in, but the rest of the kittens had to be beneath her. Danny turned his head, took a deep breath, held it, and leapt into the coop. When his foot hit, it went straight through the floor, scraping his leg. Pain rocketed through his brain, but that was the least of his problems.

He was stuck, and his breath was now gone. With the floor swallowing his leg up to the knee, he reached forward, grabbed the entire nest, and yanked it toward him.

With all his might and his last ounce of strength, he shoved the nest, Mrs. McGillicuddy and all, out the chicken door hole and onto the ramp.

His eyes and lungs burned like the roaring fire above. Only his tearing cough sounded above the crackle and howl of flames. The smoke billowed above him, pressing down like a great blanket.

Danny lay flat on his stomach, closed his eyes, and felt himself drifting away.

Danny's father stood with his arms hanging by his sides. When Danny ran to him, his father wrapped him in those beefy limbs and squeezed him until it nearly hurt.

"Let me look at you, Danny." His father held him at arm's length, looking him over. "You look good, Danny. You look strong."

"Dad, I miss you so bad."

"Oh, Danny, I miss you too, but I'm here. I'm right here with you. Always." His father put an arm around him and they began walking back from the way Danny had come. "And one day, we'll be together forever."

Danny stopped, frozen with fear, and looked up at his dad. "What do you mean?"

"Well, I'm here for you. I'm part of you. You'll hear me, but you won't see me like this. Not for a while. You've got a lot to do, you know. A whole life."

"Dad, no!" Danny grabbed his father and held him tight. "I'm not leaving you. I won't go."

"Danny, Danny, Danny. We don't choose. You're gonna be fine. I told you, I'm with you, and we will be together. I promise."

Danny didn't know what to say.

His father turned him around and let him go.

78

"Danny?"

Danny's eyes fluttered open and he saw his mom. There were tubes in his nose. His throat was chilled and dry and sore. He opened his mouth to speak.

"I saw Dad." His voice was a raspy croak.

"Oh, honey." His mom's eyes brimmed with tears. She laid her hand along his cheek. "You're here now. You're gonna be okay."

Danny looked around at the hospital room. "Who? Who got me?"

"Mr. Crenshaw." His mom bit her lip, fighting her tears, before she said, "Oh, Danny, why? Why would you do that, honey?"

"Do?" Danny looked at her as the pieces fell together in his mind, him yelling at Ms. Rait, his hint of a threat, lashing out at Mrs. McGillicuddy. It scared him silly. He shook his head. "No. No, Mom. It wasn't me. I didn't do it. Someone else did, as a prank. I went to try and stop it, but I was too late, and I tried to save Mrs. McGillicuddy and her kittens. Mom, don't look at me like that. You've got to believe me!"

She looked at the window. Their reflections were painted in ghostly images against the darkness beyond. She sighed and shook her head. "Then who? Who did it, Danny? If it wasn't you, you're gonna have to tell them who."

"Them?"

"The police." His mom nodded toward the door. "They're waiting outside."

When Danny got onto the bus Monday morning, no one cheered. Everyone went quiet and cast their eyes down, only taking secret glances his way when they thought he wasn't looking. He sat down in his usual seat halfway back. The door clattered shut and the driver revved her engine in a cloud of diesel left behind for the trees and fields to absorb.

Janey got on next. She sat right down beside him, loyal to the end. "Hey."

Danny sighed. "Hey."

Janey patted his shoulder but said nothing. They'd been through it all yesterday. She'd begged him to tell, or, at a minimum, to let her tell. Danny was having none of it.

"I can't rat out a teammate," he'd told her. "I didn't do it. If that's not enough for them, then fine. I'll never tell. And you doing it would be just like me doing it."

Janey had stood in the middle of his room and pulled at her ponytail. "They should be thanking you, Danny. You saved Mrs. McGillicuddy and those kittens. You can't miss the big game. It's just not fair. You've been dreaming about this. Look at everything you've gone through."

"I may miss the big game this year, but if I'm a rat, my football career is over in Jericho anyway. It's a team sport, Janey."

Her reply, which he couldn't argue with even now, had been, "If Bug was a real team player, he wouldn't let you be punished for something we know he did."

"I can't control Bug," he'd replied, "just me."

He wasn't surprised in the least to see Mr. Trufant waiting for him just inside the entrance to the school. They made eye contact and Danny followed him without being told. At the conference table in Mr. Trufant's office, Coach Kinen waited along with Mr. Crenshaw and, at the head of the table, Ms. Rait.

Danny sat down, folded his hands, and looked at his knuckles.

Suddenly, the door flew open and his mom rushed in and sat beside him. "I'm sorry. I had a job interview at seven thirty that I couldn't change." Danny knew that was a code for the AA meetings she'd been going to.

Mr. Trufant adjusted the tight blue knot of his tie, then cleared his throat. "That's fine, Mrs. Owens. We just sat down, and I'm sorry we have to meet again like this, but we need to chart a path forward here."

"Innocent until proven guilty," Coach Kinen barked before smacking his palm on the table. "I can't see how there's anything to discuss. Danny can't take her test under the circumstances, and we certainly can't prevent him from playing next Saturday."

Ms. Rait huffed and shook her head before muttering, "Unbelievable."

"Believe it, lady." Coach Kinen glared at the teacher.

"Let's not do this, Dave." Mr. Trufant looked scary with his bald head, steel glasses, and wrinkled brow, and he obviously wasn't afraid of Coach Kinen. "You need to let me do my job."

Coach Kinen bit his lip and nodded.

"Good," said Mr. Trufant before turning to Ms. Rait. "Martha, I will not go around you here. What happened is horrible. No one should have to go through that. It was criminal, and I'm sure the police will sort it out."

"Sort it out?" Ms. Rait scoffed. "He threatened me. He was *there.*"

Danny's mom sprang up from her seat and pointed a finger at the teacher. "If Danny says he didn't do it, he didn't do it! And he saved your cats!"

"Then who did?" Ms. Rait asked. "You can't say he doesn't know. Why would he be there? Yes, he saved the cats, after he, or someone he knows, lit a fire to destroy my property and kill my pets! Do you know those tar shingles flew hundreds of feet? They burned two acres of my neighbors' corn. What if the wind was different? My house could have burned down! If I was in bed . . ."

She brandished her crutch. "Without this? I could have been *killed*, so don't you tell me how he saved my cats!"

"Ladies, please." Mr. Trufant held up both hands. "We are

trying to work this out in the best interests of everyone here."

"That means I roll over and keep my mouth shut." Ms. Rait was steaming. "That's what that means."

"I'm sorry you feel that way, Martha. You're quite wrong." Mr. Trufant frowned at her. "If Danny turns out to be the perpetrator, he will be punished to the fullest extent of the law and within the parameters of this school district."

"Good." Ms. Rait folded her arms and sat back.

"However—"

Ms. Rait clucked her tongue and rolled her eyes. "Oh, however."

"Yes. However." Mr. Trufant spoke calmly and quietly, and it somehow made his words more powerful. "It is a fundamental right in our country that people are presumed innocent. I do not want to punish someone who not only may have done nothing wrong, but who may have done something very right. So, I am recommending that we suspend Danny from your class and that we allow him to play this Saturday, unless he is found to be guilty before that. But—let me finish—I will not implement this plan unless you agree."

"Unless *I* agree?" Ms. Rait pointed to herself.

"Yes." Mr. Trufant nodded. "If you don't agree, we'll have to come up with an alternative."

The room went quiet.

Outside, Danny could hear the rumble and muted chatter of his classmates getting ready for the day.

Finally, Ms. Rait spoke. "Okay, I'll tell you what I will agree to . . ."

"Everything stays the same." Ms. Rait looked around the table. "It is true that we should presume innocence. So, we'll carry on like this never happened."

Danny smiled at his mom. She gave him a one-armed hug.

"Nice," said Coach Kinen.

"Danny will take my test in third period like everyone else. If he passes, he plays. If not . . . well, they're your rules, Mr. Trufant."

"Wait. What?" Coach Kinen was out of his seat. "You can't be impartial grading his test. We know you think he did it."

"It's a multiple-choice test, Coach Kinen." Ms. Rait had a blank face. "There's no subjectivity to it at all."

Danny sat, stunned. He hadn't seen this coming. She knew he probably couldn't pass. He felt like she'd tricked them all.

It was Monday, so when Danny reported to the library for study hall, they sent him to Mr. Crenshaw's office.

Danny dreaded it, but he was in no position to skip a session or do anything else outside the lines. He knocked, then entered.

Mr. C looked up from his computer and stopped typing. "Hi, Danny."

Danny stopped just inside the door. "I can go back to the library if you don't want me. They said you just have to write me a pass."

Mr. C frowned. "Why would I not want you?"

"Seriously?" Danny searched his face.

Mr. C shrugged. "This weekend has nothing to do with what we do here. I thought you'd know that by now."

Danny narrowed his eyes. "I guess."

Mr. C pointed at the couch. "Sit. Make yourself comfortable. Do you want to talk?"

Danny slowly crossed the floor and sat, keeping his eyes on Mr. C all the while. "I don't know. Do you?"

"Sure. We can talk, or you can study."

Danny didn't care if he sounded bitter. "It's too late for that."

"Really? I heard you were so close."

"From who? Ms. Rait?" Danny wrinkled his face.

"Yes. She has confidence in you." Mr. C pointed a pen at him.

"That makes no sense. She told me it didn't look good."

"She's challenging you, Danny, like a coach. She asked me how I thought she should approach you with all this and I told her back in the beginning that you'd respond best if she approached it like a coach. You're used to that. You've responded well to that all your life." Mr. C held up both hands like it was a simple fact.

Danny didn't know what to say.

"I told her she'd have to be careful to mix in praise and encouragement, too. I hope she did that. Did she?" Mr. C asked.

Danny had to nod because she had done that. It was he who'd focused on the negative and allowed it to overshadow her kindnesses and encouragement. He looked up and blinked. "So she *wants* me to pass?"

Mr. Crenshaw wore a sad smile. "So very much."

"And she thinks I can?"

"No, Danny." Mr. C shook his head. "She thinks you *will*."

ONE WEEK LATER...

The air had that late-fall bite, but the sun shining down between the big-bellied gray clouds made it the perfect day for football.

Danny looked through his facemask across the field at Dillon Junior High's green jerseys. Their defensive line was enormous.

"What you looking at?" Cupcake bumped up against Danny's shoulder pads.

"They're pretty huge," Danny said.

"Biggest junior high D-line in Texas, they say." Cupcake spit on the turf. "Can't say we won't miss Bug."

"Yeah." Danny waited to see what else his friend had to say.

"Makes you kinda proud, though, him owning up like he did. No one told him he had to, either."

"Yeah. I'm glad he did."

Cupcake waved a big, taped-up paw high and wide. "Everyone knew it wasn't you."

"Ms. Rait didn't," Danny said.

"I guess she turned out okay. Didn't she?" Cupcake said. "That letter she wrote. No one could believe it. I mean, she won't press charges if he gets counseling. Go figure."

"We don't know what the police will do," Danny said. "It's nice of her to try, though."

"Yeah, and she passed you, too. If she hadn't done that, we'd be in real hot water right now."

"Hey. *I* passed that test, not her. A solid seventy-two."

"Well . . . give us an A-plus today and we just might win this thing." Cupcake bumped Danny's fist and jogged off toward the end zone where the linemen were gathering.

Danny watched him go, then looked up and scanned the press box. Sitting in a neat row were the Jericho varsity coaches, the men who'd either make his dream come true or shatter it. Ms. Rait would argue it was Danny who'd make or break the dream, and he nodded to himself that that was true.

He had to play out of his mind today. It wasn't about Coach Oglethorpe—with his bucket hat and the black mustache and goatee beneath those heavy dark sunglasses—or his nine assistants. It was about Daniel Owens playing with the heart and skill of another Daniel Owens, some thirty years ago, on this same field. He knew this afternoon that's exactly what was going to happen.

From the press box, his eyes traveled into the stands where his mom sat with Janey, Ms. Rait, and Mr. Crenshaw. He waved, and his mom waved back. He knew her eyes never left him, and that made him think about his father.

Danny still didn't know if he'd just dreamed about seeing his dad or if he'd actually died and come back. Either way, his father's words stayed with him, and he knew they would for the rest of his life.

I'm here. I'm right here with you. Always.

AUTHOR'S NOTE

In my own middle grade years growing up, the world was quite different. Kids with special needs were separated from the rest of us, and anyone in need of mental health counseling was secretly labeled "crazy" and avoided like a mortal disease.

Fortunately, thankfully, things have gotten much better, although we still have work to do. While this is a football story full of touchdowns and tackles, grand victories and crushing defeats, it is also very much a story about mental health and how, with treatment and time, people can—and many times do—get better. To make the interactions and the outcomes with Mr. Crenshaw accurate, I relied on my oldest son, Thane, who is a licensed family therapist with a master's degree in mental health counseling for adolescents and kids. And, as Mr. Crenshaw does with Danny (and hopefully Bug), my son

Thane often helps kids get better and alter the paths of their lives.

It is the job for the rest of us to understand that mental health is a serious problem that can affect any one of us or our family members and to be kind and compassionate toward those who need help. Finally, I want to mention that for accuracy, I worked closely with Connie Bohrer, a wonderful teacher and reading specialist, on the details of Danny's reading impairment and the process and timing of bringing him up to speed in just eight weeks.

Thank you to Thane and Connie and also my editor, Karen Chaplin, for her careful scrutiny and advice on both these important issues!

And if you need help, or know of someone who does, please contact the National Suicide Hotline at 1-800-SUICIDE (1-800-784-2433) or the National Suicide Prevention Lifeline at 1-800-273-TALK (1-800-273-8255).

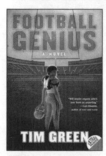

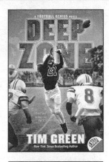
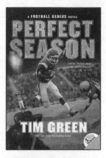

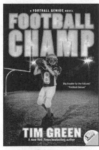

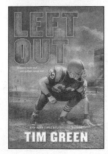
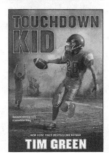